Watch Me TakeOff

Also by
Ilona Duncan

My Jewish Great Grandmother

At Home on the Road

www.ilonaduncan.com

Watch Me Take Off

The Life of Ian J. (Jim) Duncan

By Ilona Duncan

First Edition Copyright 2022 Ilona Duncan

All rights reserved. No part of this book may be reproduced in any form or by any means, electronic, graphic, or mechanical, including photocopying, recording, or by any information storage retrieval systems, without permission in writing by the author.

Printed in the United States of America

ISBN 978-0-578-38437-5

Library of Congress Control Number: 2022904168

This book was designed and produced
by Hearth & Garden Productions

A. Cort Sinnes, Design

Cover photograph: *"Sky Trail,"* © 2021 Creative Commons

Aviation in itself is not inherently dangerous. But to an even greater degree than the sea, it is terribly unforgiving of any carelessness, incapacity, or neglect.

Captain Alfred Gilmer Lamplugh
RAF pilot in World War I
Principle Surveyor of The British Aviation Insurance Co., Ltd.

Author's Foreword

In 2019, I completed *At Home on the Road*, a book that tells the story of Ian and I wandering around North America in a converted Marathon bus. After that wondrous experience from 1999 to 2001, and having moved to the Northern Neck of Virginia, we enjoyed taking cruises. We had not lost our adventurous spirits to see the world. The spring of 2020, Ian looked forward to a six-week-cruise around the Pacific, hoping to revisit islands we had seen forty-five years earlier. Covid-19 made this impossible and kept us at home. That's when I decided to write a book about Ian's life.

I bought an audio recorder, scheduled daily interviews, and urged Ian to recall past events. Over the following months, Ian relived his childhood, youth, and an aviation career that spanned 47 years. Ian turned 85 in 2020, and despite his advanced age, he had a stellar memory. In detail, he recalled names and past events. To authenticate Ian's story, I went through files of memorabilia and extracted photos, documents, speeches, and letters. A heavy folder held all his military flight records. There were also Ian's eight flight logbooks, in which he recorded every private and commercial flight: from his 1951 solo in a Piper J-3, to his 1988 final landing in a Pan American Boeing 747.

During the year-long process, anecdotes turned into chapters, which Ian read carefully. He made suggestions and corrected possible misconceptions. Once or twice, I noticed a quiet sniffle when Ian read a passage from his youth. "This is beautiful," he said. Then Ian's health deteriorated. In the spring of 2021, I worried time was running out, that Ian might not live long enough for me to finish his book. That's when my friend and editor, Gail Kenna, suggested I change my process. Instead of writing and editing, I took notes while Ian spoke. The point finally arrived when I knew most of the story because from 1970 onward, I was part of his life.

Ian looked forward to the book, my gift to him when we could no longer travel. *Watch Me Take Off* is also a gift to family members, our children, and grandchildren, so they can appreciate the legacy of Ian J. Duncan. He was a man from a generation that believed in humility, integrity, personal responsibility, and hard work. Lastly, I hope anyone enamored with aviation will find pleasure in reading about a past era of joyous and adventurous flying.

All eight of Ian's flight logbooks, in which he recorded every private and commercial flight in his forty-seven-year career.

1

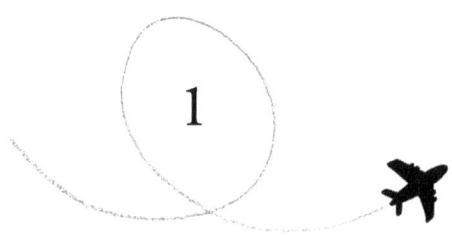

Ian, a lanky teenager at seventeen kneels beside a Piper J-3 Cub. No wonder his friends nicknamed him *The Rake*. He and I would not meet until eighteen years later, when we worked for Pan American World Airways. Love of travel and flight brought us together; and in 1974 we married. Now, in 2021, I am writing the memoir of Ian James Duncan, an aviator at a time when commercial flight was gaining popularity and advancing toward the jet age.

Ian's story begins one sunny afternoon in 1949. He remembers that June day well, leaving the Butler Country Club on his new Monarch bike with its horns and light, a bicycle bought with his own money from caddying. In his pocket were five quarters, his earnings that day. The money would go to his mother for safekeeping in a small chamois leather purse. "Mom was thrifty," Ian often told me, rolling the 'r' in memory of her Scottish burr. But in 1949, fourteen-year-old Ian hoped there would be enough money in her purse to buy clothes before ninth grade began in September.

The road home passed the Butler-Graham Airport, with *Scholter Aviation* in big lettering on a hangar. Something prompted Ian to stop that day, which wasn't his habit. He recalls turning onto a narrow road toward the hangars and having to stop. A telephone pole had been placed across the path to prevent cars from entering the airfield. With one foot on the pedal, the other foot against the pole, Ian watched planes circle the field, land, and take off again. Before long, a man left the hangar and walked in Ian's direction. The man's attire, a long-sleeve shirt with a bowtie, caught Ian's attention. Introducing himself as Ken Scholter, he said he remembered Ian, knew he was the son of T.W. Phillips' chauffeur. Ian dismounted the bike to shake hands with Mr. Scholter, who commented on how much Ian had grown since he last saw him. That had been three years before, the day of Ian's first airplane ride.

As Ian tells the story, one Saturday morning in May 1946, when the Duncans were having breakfast, his father announced that Roger Philips, T.W.'s 24-four-year-old son, was giving him a ride in his new plane. Eleven-year-old Ian wanted to be invited, but he was aware of his parents' subservient position on the estate. No point asking his dad for permission to tag along. So, Ian devised his own ploy. After breakfast, he went outside, hid behind some bushes, and watched for Roger's convertible to appear on the road. When it did, with Roger and his father inside, Ian ran toward the car, calling, "Where are you going?" Roger told Ian to hop in and come along. As Ian recalls, the plane was a four-seater, single engine Fairchild-24. He sat in the back and watched how Roger pulled the plane up into a clear sky. As the plane circled over Butler and headed for Pittsburgh and back, Ian saw houses below and traffic on Route 8. He wondered if one day he could learn to fly.

Now, three years later, beside his bicycle, Ian heard Mr. Scholter ask if he worked. Ian said he caddied at the golf course when work was available. Mr. Scholter needed some help at the airport and offered Ian a job: to cut grass, push planes in and out, gas them up, wash windshields, and assist the mechanic. The work would be on weekends, full-time in summer. Ian would receive the minimum wage, seventy cents an hour. Five dollars, sixty cents a day, Ian calculated. A goldmine! Too good to be true. His new bike had depleted his savings. He asked how soon he could start. Mr. Scholter said to come the following morning.

Ian rode off, pedaling faster than ever, eager to tell his mother about the new job. He recalls that she stood by the stove and, without looking at him, asked if he had been offered some menial tasks for Roger Phillips and his wife. Recently, they had hired Ian's older sister, Helen, as a babysitter. Not until Ian described his encounter with Mr. Scholter and the wage he would earn, did Isabella realize that her wee boy, who used to sing in the church choir, had suddenly grown up. However, Ian was a minor, and his parents needed to sign a work permit, which required the approval of the county clerk. But that could wait a few weeks.

The following morning, Ian arrived at the Butler-Graham

Airport, also known as Pittsburgh-Butler Airport, eager to begin his new job. That day in 1949 determined his destiny as a pilot who would fly airplanes.

2

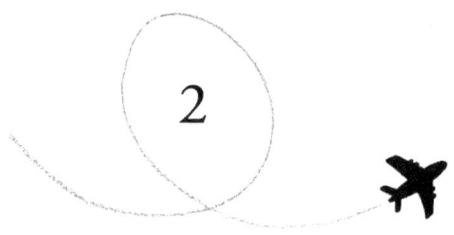

Ian James Millar was the second child of George Duncan and Isabella Brownlee. Both were born in 1900 in Edinburgh. The two had been high school sweethearts. Isabella, orphaned young and raised by an aunt, became an office clerk in Edinburgh.

George, age 22, worked as a typesetter. Yet his income was meager, with little chance for advancement. His employer suggested that George immigrate to the United States and even loaned him seventy pounds, about three-hundred dollars. George accepted, said he would pay the loan back with interest, which he did five years later. A third-class steamship ticket from Liverpool to Boston cost eighteen pounds (80 dollars). This left George enough money for living expenses until he secured a job in the New World. On March 2nd, 1923, at the Edinburgh train station, before boarding a train to Liverpool, George bade farewell to his parents, brothers, sister, and Isabella.

Isabella Brownlee, c. 1920.

The following day, George and 900 other emigrants boarded the *Andania II*, a recently launched 14,000-ton Cunard Ocean liner, and left Liverpool's harbor. If there was sadness leaving his home country, George, by his own account, hid his feelings. According to his onboard diary, he amused himself singing and dancing during the twelve-day crossing. On occasion he dressed in collar and tie to visit the second-class smokeroom. In his diary he never mentioned his fiancé, his family, or his sadness about leaving home. He did write, "Anything was better than letting my mind dwell on the subject, which was apt to bring a lump to my throat."

In Boston, George initially worked for a watch company. Yet he kept scanning newspaper want-ads for a better-paying job. Then an unusual advertisement caught his eye: Chauffeur needed; contact T. W. Phillips Jr., Butler, Pennsylvania. I doubt George had heard of Butler, a town 35 miles north of Pittsburgh. Yet Mr. Phillips' offer tempted him. An increase in pay and free housing. He traveled by train and bus to Butler, accepted the position, and asked Isabella to join him.

George and Isabella at the Edinburgh train station, 1923.

George and Isabella were married in New York City. A professional 1929 studio portrait shows Isabella in a white organdy dress and matching bonnet, holding a large bouquet of chrysanthemums. George looks elegant in a dark-vested suit, a white carnation in his left lapel, and shoes with white-button spats.

Isabella and George's wedding photo, New York City, 1929.

I can only guess Isabella's thoughts about moving to Butler. No doubt it was her love for George that made her leave family and friends for an unknown place. What would have been her first impression of Phillips Hall? Did she feel privileged? Humbled? I imagine the young couple compared the Phillips' mansion to a Scottish manor house, and regarded T.W. Phillips as a wealthy local *laird,* and his wife as Lady Alma.

Thomas Wharton Phillips Jr. was the president of *T. W. Phillips Gas and Oil,* a family-owned enterprise that supplied natural gas and oil to local industries like ARMCO (American Rolling Mill Company), a steel manufacturer. Phillips Hall, noted as one of America's most spectacular private homes, was a 46-room Tudor-Gothic mansion, designed by the well-known Pittsburgh architect, Benno Janssen. Records show the cost was one million dollars at its completion in 1929. Built with red brick, the house had two elevators, sixteen bedrooms and baths, a formal library, and a large ballroom, which held a built-in Skinner pipe organ with mechanical parts that filled two basement rooms. Besides a chauffeur, the Phillips family employed a staff of servants: maids, groundkeepers, butler, primary chef, sous-chef, kitchen helpers, a laundress.

The property itself encompassed 125 acres of forests, fields, and several dependencies. An important landmark was a brick-enclosed water tower, 100 feet high. Its tanks held approximately 10,000 gallons of potable well water, which also served to extinguish fires. Sheep grazed in the fields, fruit trees produced apples, peaches, pears. A devoted arborist, Mr. Phillips planted a species of every tree native to Pennsylvania. Lilacs bloomed in the spring, and a flower garden held varieties of roses, daffodils, dahlias, tulips. Ian thinks there were enough flowers for a thousand bouquets.

George and Isabella moved into a furnished apartment above the Phillips' brick carriage house, a thousand feet from the mansion. When Ian and I visited the estate in 2006, the house looked much the same from the outside as Ian remembered it. A photo from our visit shows five closed-in bays. Ian said three had been for the Phillips' cars, the other two served as a laundry room with washing machines and dryers, plus a large frame to stretch curtains to size. Above were the windows of the Duncan's apartment. The lower back level, not seen in the photo, had six more bays for cars belonging to the

The Phillips' carriage house in 2006.

Phillips' children. All of them had vehicles at sixteen, Ian recalls.

That day in August 2006, the estate appeared abandoned. We entered the Phillips' mansion unnoticed, walked through the entry hall with its wide curved staircase, the dining room, and library. I could tell that Ian felt uncomfortable inside the house he was not allowed to enter as a young boy, and he was eager to leave. I suggested visiting the carriage house. Its entry door was unlocked, and I was first to climb the old staircase to what had been the Duncan's living quarters. Reluctantly, Ian followed. Upstairs we entered a large room with tables, chairs, and scattered bric-a-brac. "Looks like someone has turned the place into a bar," Ian said. (Later, while researching the estate's history, I learned that the apartment had been converted to a nightclub in the late 1970s.) Ian and I stood where the living room had been. I imagined Ian's father reading or listening to the wireless, his mother mending clothes. When asked about the furnishings, Ian could not remember. This did not surprise me. For as long as I've known Ian, he hasn't shown interest in home décor. No sign of a kitchen, just a double door that opened to the old balcony. We hesitated to step out for fear it might be unsafe. Ian told me his parents had left the estate in 1956, not long after T.W. Phillips Jr. died.

I was glad for the visit and now able to picture where Ian's parents began their married life in 1929. Ian's father maintained the Phillips' eight cars, chauffeured Mr. Phillips, and ran errands for the family. When the Phillips entertained, Isabella occasionally worked as a head server. "Always a lavish affair," Ian explained. And because his mother could type and take steno, she worked as Alma Phillips' on-call secretary, paid by the day. Ian estimated his father's monthly wage at one hundred dollars.

On January 23rd, 1930, Ian's parents became members of Butler's First Presbyterian Church. From that day and until old age, their lives revolved around the Christian calendar: the birth of their children, baptisms, confirmations, and eventual weddings. George sang in the church choir and joined the Butler Musical Society, which later became the Butler County Symphony Association. When Mr. Phillips became aware of George's and Isabella's love for music and, whenever he and his wife were unable to attend the Pittsburgh Symphony Orchestra or the Pittsburgh Opera, he offered his seats to them.

In 1932, the Duncans welcomed their first child, a daughter, and named her Helen Jean. Ian James Millar arrived January 17th, 1935, followed by sister Isobel in 1937. Millar was Ian's paternal grandmother's maiden name. In 1939, George made his first return to Scotland and took four-year-old Ian to meet his grandparents. Fears of war breaking out in Europe might have hastened George's decision. Today, Ian speculates that

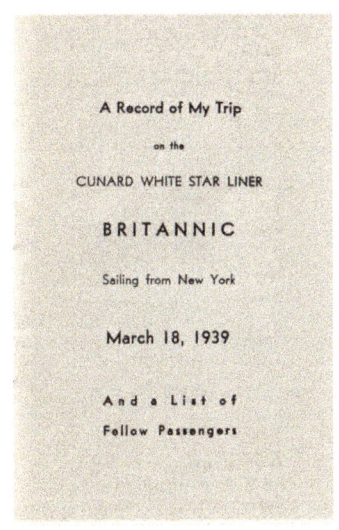

Mr. Phillips urged his father to visit his family and paid their round-trip fares.

On March 18th, 1939, Ian and his father sailed from New York to England on Cunard's *Britannic*. At four, Ian was too young to recall details of their voyage. Mr. G. Duncan and Master I. Duncan are listed in a commemorative booklet with the names of each passenger.

Father and son spent two weeks in Scotland before they boarded the *Queen Mary* on April 15th and sailed from Southampton to New York. As a memento, his grandparents gave Ian a book that described the Scottish clans and tartans, a gift Ian cherished throughout his life. In

Ian with his grandfather William Fox Duncan in Edinburgh, 1939.

time, Ian learned that the Duncans belonged to the Robertson clan. Ian did not see his grandparents again. Ann, Ian's grandmother, then 73, died in 1941 and her husband, William Fox Duncan in 1947.

Above: *A book on Scottish clans and their tartans was a gift from Ian's grandparents. From it, Ian learned that "Nemo Me Impune Lacessit" (No one provokes me with impunity) was Scotland's motto.* Below: *From the same book, Ian learned that his family was a member of the Clan Robertson.*

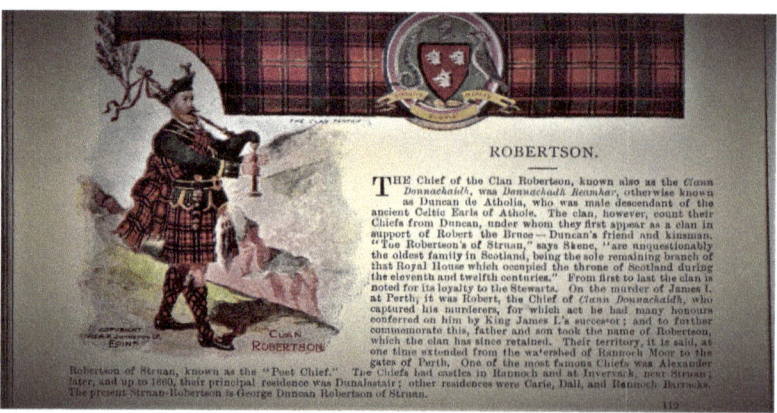

Isabella and George waited 25 years, until 1966, to make one last trip to the old country. George had been granted U.S. citizenship on June 8th, 1932, at Common Pleas Court in Butler. Isabella became a U.S citizen on December 6th, 1939. Yet at heart they remained Scottish, attended annual picnics and Scottish festivals, and memorized Robert Burns' poetry. A favorite at mealtimes was:

Some hae meat and canna eat,
And some wad eat that want it,
But we hae meat, and we can eat,
Sae let the Lord be thankit

Isabella and George, 1948.

3

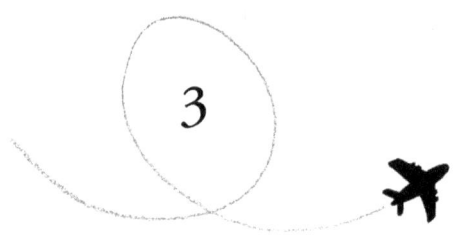

Helen, Isobel, and Ian knew their parents were servants on the estate and revered the Phillips' family as royalty. Warned to be polite always, the Duncan siblings were not allowed near the mansion, guesthouse, and pool. After T.W. Phillips' son, Roger, married and built a separate house on the estate, Ian and his sisters knew to keep away from it. Yet they were free to play in the meadows and wander the forests, or help their mother pick wild strawberries and blackberries, which she made into jam. And the Duncans were given a small plot for growing vegetables. Ian recalls aiding his father annually to prepare the soil, plant seeds, and water tomatoes, peppers, cucumbers, carrots, beets, lettuce, and cabbages. What the family did not consume was canned.

Ian was a curious child, and curiosity often got him in trouble, which resulted in a sore seat. He was between seven and eight when he nearly started a fire on the estate. That day he and Isobel gathered a pile of leaves near the tennis courts. In wanting to impress his sister, Ian intended to burn them, took a long wooden match from his pocket, and struck it on a stone. Luck had it that a nearby groundskeeper was watching the two children. Seeing the match in the boy's hand, he yelled and hurried toward them, then berated Ian and took the match away. He told Ian to go home immediately and tell his parents. At home, his dad removed his belt and made sure Ian never played with matches or fire again.

There was a mischievous incident at the apple orchard, too. Ian and Isobel had gone with their mother to pick apples. Helen, Ian's older sister, stayed home that day. She knew by then to elude her brother's company for fear of the trouble he might cause. While his mother filled a basket of apples, Ian noticed what looked like a bee buzzing in and out of a hole in the ground. For a few seconds he stood there, wondering about the hole and what had attracted the insect to it. He motioned Isobel to come over, picked up a small green apple from the ground, and dropped it down the hole. Underground, a nest of wasps took the apple as an act of war, stormed out, ready to attack. Ian ran for his life and avoided a sting. Isobel, too scared to move, could only scream. Stung multiple times, she required

Above: *Ian with sisters Helen and Isobel, Phillips Estate.* Right: *Ian and Isobel.*

medical attention. Ian, in his own words, caught hell for that prank. And for years Isobel talked about it.

Ian thinks he was a bad eight-year-old rascal, a lonely boy with too much free time, particularly during summer recess. It so happened that during summer, senior groundkeepers hired local high school kids to help mow, plant, and maintain flower beds. The teenagers also tilled around Mr. Phillips' prized trees, breaking the ground into fine soil so it absorbed more water. Ian, for lack of a playmate was eager to socialize. Already at a young age, he longed for an audience, wanted to entertain, be heard, a characteristic that later served him well. That summer on the estate, Ian sheepishly hung around and pestered the older kids with childish questions: *What are you doing? Where do you live? You have a girlfriend?* Irritated with the eight-year-old chatterbox, they repeatedly told Ian to shut up and get lost. That's when Ian turned snooty and bragged that he lived on the estate. Threatened with a shovel, Ian ran away. Then one day, he recognized a summer hire as Bob McCall, the son of his mother's friend. Ian ran up to Bob and asked what he was doing there. Bob snapped at Ian and said to leave him alone. Ian kept badgering him until Bob yelled, "Go home to your mother." That's when Ian sassed back. He said that he had heard about Bob's father hanging around *Plainview*, a local watering hole. Later that day, Bob told his mother that Ian had called Mr. McCall a drunk. Word soon reached Isabella. She went into a rage. No matter that Ian denied the charge, or whether the account was true or false, Ian had caused his mother embarrassment. This was far worse than what he had or had not done. "Once again, all hell broke loose. I didn't sit for a day."

Yet there were happy moments. Of the many Phillips'

servants, the French chef found a way to Ian's heart and his stomach. Ian still remembers Auguste le Cann, dressed in the traditional white double-breasted jacket, black-and-white hounds tooth pants, and *toque blanche.* When Ian's father returned from town with the chef's requested items, Ian was the one who met Mr. le Cann at one of the mansion's employee entrances. The chef spoke with a heavy accent and was difficult to understand. But always he had a treat for Ian. On the occasion whenever Mr. le Cann came to the garage to fetch one of the cars for a trip to buy gourmet provisions in Pittsburgh, he had with him cookies for Ian and his sisters.

In 1940, Ian attended the Penn Township Elementary School. He was five, the youngest in a class of seven boys and five girls. George and Isabella, fearing the older kids might torment their wee lad, told Ian to alert the teacher if any bullying occurred. But rather than be a tattletale, Ian learned to defend himself. He walked the mile and a half to the two-room building. First grade and second were in one room, third and fourth in the other. School began at eight. During the warmer months, the classrooms smelled old and musty. In winter, a coal-burning stove exuded a sulfuric, bituminous odor. Each pupil brought his or her own lunch which was eaten at their desks. Ian recalls his lunch as a bologna, cheese, or peanut butter-jelly sandwich, a piece of fruit, a container of watered-down juice, and, on occasion, a cookie. The students were allowed two play periods. That's when they used the wooden outhouse toilet. Before the start of each new school year, the outhouse was relocated to a new pit. But by the following summer, the toilet's stench permeated the schoolyard. During winter, the children took turns feeding coal into the potbelly stove and removing the ashes. On very cold mornings, everyone kept their coats on because the classroom did not reach a comfortable temperature until second or third period. Stove duty was also a punishment for misbehavior. A latecomer or interrupter had to tote buckets of coal for several days. Ian said he always behaved in the classroom. His father had warned him that any word from the school better be good news.

During his pubescence, Ian agonized that his family was poor. He envied schoolmates who wore new clothes at the start of each schoolyear. In patched knickers, handmade socks, and sweaters, he felt embarrassed. Children teased him for wearing the same tennis shoes all year. In winter, he lined them with newspapers to keep his socks from getting wet. And Helen's rubber galoshes were passed down to Ian after his father used an inner tube kit to repair a tear. The main reason Ian wanted to work was to have better shoes and clothes, so he would not appear to be the son of a poor immigrant.

One of his earliest responsibilities, before caddying at the golf course, was to shine shoes. Ian cannot remember if Mr. Phillips or his butler offered the job. Every three or four days before school, Ian entered the mansion's utility room, wiped dirt off the shoes, polished them, and placed the clean ones on a table. Someone, probably the butler, kept score of the number he cleaned. The money, a dollar for seven pairs, went straight into his mother's chamois purse for safekeeping.

From an early age, Ian and his sisters helped with chores around the house. They set the table and took turns washing and drying dishes. Ian's favorite task was to help his father wash the Phillips' cars. One by one, the cars were moved from their parking stalls to the washing bay with its hot and cold water, buckets, whisk brooms, sponges, and white-wall tire cleaner. To wash each vehicle required the better part of an hour. This included wiping the surface with a chamois cloth to avoid water marks and, if needed, simonizing by hand. At twelve, after he learned to drive his father's 1940 four-door sedan, Ian was allowed to move a Phillips' car in and out of the wash bay.

At eleven, Ian also trapped rabbits for Mr. Phillips, who wanted to diminish the rabbit population. They had become a nuisance, particularly in winter, and gnawed bark from the estate's trees. A Pennsylvania game warden provided Ian with fifteen wooden traps. Each morning before sunrise, Ian checked them and placed the caught rabbits in cages. The Game Warden fetched the animals once a week and released them on public land. A few fat ones, however, made it into

A young Ian with four of the Phillips' cars, Phillips Estate, c. 1942.

Above: *Buick Limousine Series 60.* Below: *Jorndan Great Line Model 90 Coupe.*

the Duncan's kitchen. One of Mr. Phillips' groundkeepers had shown Ian how to land a fatal blow to a rabbit's neck, killing it instantly. He also showed Ian how to skin and clean the animal. With a facetious grin, Ian says, "We ate many rabbits."

The Duncan's meager finances did not preclude a summer vacation. In 1946, Ian's parents rented a cabin for a week at *Presque Isle State Park* on Lake Erie. By then Ian knew how to swim. He claimed no formal instruction and said he learned by going with school buddies to the swimming holes of Thorn Creek, half a mile from the estate. Ian has no notable recollection of the trip to Lake Erie, except that he was allowed to spend a few dimes and nickels on rides at nearby *Waldameer Amusement Park*. But he recalls summer vacations in Ocean City, New Jersey. Regardless of the sunburn he and his sisters suffered the first year, Ian treasured the beach, ocean, and waves. Plus, at a Boardwalk shack, Ian had his first taste of fish and chips. At the time he thought that nothing could ever taste better.

Christian holidays and birthdays were *en famille*. His parents could not afford parties or provide cake to a bunch of kids, Ian told me. The family's Thanksgiving turkey came from a local farm, and at Christmas Ian's mother roasted a large chicken. Scottish haggis never made the Duncan's table, as Ian's father was not fond of the dish. Yet the family loved Isabella's shortbread and apple pies. To prevent the summer's apples from spoilage, they were stored inside the estate's water

Photo from the Butler Eagle, *January 26, 1946, shows 11-year-old Ian in front row, far left.*

tower. It also accommodated a 100-hundred-pound burlap bag of potatoes, bought for five dollars. And with ingredients shipped from Scotland, Ian's mother baked fruitcake and mince pie for Christmas, a tradition Ian fancied throughout life. The children helped place ornaments on a spruce, cut fresh on the Phillips' property. After a musical church service on Christmas Eve, with Ian and his sisters in the choir, the family opened gifts on Christmas morning. Mr. Phillips gave all three children an envelope with a new one-dollar bill, raised to five dollars by the time Ian was a teenager.

In the Duncan household, the three children were taught morals and manners. Years later, I recall my mother-in-law mentioning the importance of the table manners she had been taught in the old country. Every Sunday, the family attended church. Ian's father was a church elder and sang in the choir. Further emphasis was on a good education. All three children learned a musical instrument: Helen played piano and organ, Isobel piano, and Ian violin. And Mr. Phillips, to entice George to remain his chauffeur, established an educational trust fund of five thousand dollars for each of the children. The funds were in blue chip stocks, the accounts held at the Union Trust in Butler, a bank T.W. Phillips started in 1929. By the time Ian and his sisters began college, their funds had grown to $25,000 each (250,000 in today's money).

This professional photo shows the family dressed in their Sunday best. Ian does not remember the occasion, possibly Easter in 1942, when he was seven. Helen, to his left, had just turned ten, and Isobel would be five within three months. A

Family photograph, c. 1942.

photo session at a studio would have been costly and required a special purpose. Nowadays, people have phones to take shots and selfies, post them an instant later. But then, fewer than 100 years ago, Ian's parents paid for a family portrait, and mailed it to Scotland to share their well-being with relatives.

Ian grew up financially poor but rich in love. He was proud of his parents and held them in high esteem. In later years, after he became successful, Ian did not mask his childhood with its simple upbringing. He always spoke lovingly of his parents parents, who taught him humility, politeness, and strong values.

Helen, Ian and Isobel, c. 1947.

4

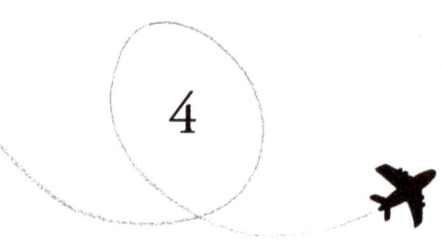

In June 1949, the night before Ian's first workday at Scholter Aviation, he lay awake, overly excited about the semi-permanent job at the airport. His mind wandered to the times he had spent on the estate's water tower, watching planes land and take-off a mile to the west. Airmail drop and pickup was a special thrill. Across the runway, a postal worker erected two vertical 30-foot steel poles 60 feet apart, then attached the mail sack to a horizontal line between the poles.

Painting of an AAA (All American Aviation) Stinson Reliant. Artist unknown.

Ian remembers how the plane, a wide-winged scarlet Stinson Reliant, dragged a line with a hook and passed by the tower, close enough for him to see inside the cockpit. In memory he recalls watching as the plane buzzed the runway at roughly 60 feet, dropped its mail container, snagged the mail sack, and flew away. Yet air traffic was not the only attraction that made Ian climb the staircase inside the water tower. Up there he had a view of young ladies swimming in and lounging around the Phillips' Olympic-size pool. Sometimes they were topless. Considering the era, I questioned bare-breasted. Ian insisted this was not an imagined sight.

That June night, sleep eventually came. And the following morning Ian arrived early at the Butler-Graham airport's administrative offices. The secretary announced that Ian Duncan was there to see Mr. Scholter. Ian remembers the office, with medals and pictures on the walls. A photo with Charles Lindbergh caught his attention and he asked about it. Mr. Scholter said he had been a sixteen-year-old kid, working at Bettis Field near Pittsburgh the summer of 1927, when he met Coronel Lindbergh, who had completed his historic transatlantic flight. On a cross-country tour, Lindbergh landed his *Spirit of St. Louis* at Bettis Field. Little did Ian know that years later he would meet Charles Lindbergh on a Pan American flight from New York to the Paris Air Show.

That June morning, Mr. Scholter's kind-hearted smile made Ian feel at ease. "I always liked the man," he told me. Ian met Scholter's manager, James Cronenwett, whose office was next door, before being led to the hangar. The multitude of planes, roughly twenty models, astounded Ian. He shook hands with Richard George, the senior of two mechanics. Both were Army Air Corps veterans from the Second World War, as Ian later learned. Outside the hangar, few planes were on the field.

The 1974 photo from the Butler Eagle *shows Ken Scholter at 64 holding the newspaper clipping about his encounter with Charles Lindbergh.*

Mr. Scholter explained that given Butler's weather, most aircraft owners wanted their planes inside, which meant the two hangars were usually full. This included Scholter's six Piper J-3 training aircraft. That morning, Ian received instructions on handling the planes and using the gas pumps. Mr. Scholter said he would watch Ian for several days and answer any of his questions.

A few days later, Ian happened to be in Hangar One. Richard George asked him to go to Hangar Two and fetch a bucket of prop wash. Ian hurried to the second hangar, searched high and low, but could not locate the item. An aircraft owner, working on his plane, noticed Ian looking around and asked if he was missing something. Ian said he had been told to get a bucket of prop wash. The man smirked, shrugged his shoulders, said he had not seen it. Frustrated, Ian returned to Hangar One and saw some students and instructors standing with Mr. Scholter.

"Where is it?" Richard George wanted to know. Ian, feeling apologetic, said that he could not find the bucket. Everyone broke out in laughter. Ian had fallen for the classic aviation prank. For anyone who does not know the joke, prop wash is the disturbed air mass pushed back by an airplane's propeller. (I didn't know the joke either!).

The summer of 1949, Ian spent most of his time at the airport. The field remained open from dawn to dusk and, depending on the needs of aircraft owners, Ian worked ten to twelve-hour shifts. Each morning he unlocked the metal cabinets that held the fuel pumps and engine oils. Then he studied the training schedule and pulled the appropriate planes from hangars. Ian handled the small Piper Cubs alone. Larger planes, like a Stinson Reliant or Navion, required three persons: one on each wing, and a third to manually steer the nose wheel. Ian also readied the planes for the student pilot and instructor. The planes that returned from flights required refueling. And their bellies had to be cleaned with Varsol liquid and all windshields wiped. In a logbook, Ian recorded the amount of fuel used. At day's end, he returned the logbook to the office. Whenever it was necessary, Ian replaced the outside rope tie-down lines, swept grass and dirt from the hangar, and made sure that oil leakage from radial engines dripped into pans, not on the floor.

If he had a break, Ian used the time to climb inside a plane, sit at the controls, and imagine the thrill of flying. Soon he could identify the different makes and models: Piper J-3, Piper PA-12 Super Cruiser, Stinson Voyager, Ryan Navion, Taylorcraft, Cessnas (140, 170,195), Aeroncas, Ercoupes. Most were privately owned. The Michael T. Baker Engineering Company kept a Stinson Stable Wing Reliant at the Butler-Graham airfield. Gulf Oil had a Stinson Gullwing Reliant there. Both planes were operated by corporate pilots. Bill Riley, the chief pilot for U.S. Steel, flew their Super DC-3 into Butler-Graham quarterly to be washed and cleaned. Ian thinks it was a high paying contract because everyone helped with this plane, even Mr. Scholter.

Every two weeks, Ian mowed the field with a Farmall tractor and, once a year he painted the bright yellow cones that marked the airport's boundaries. Ian knew he had to work diligently because an opportunity like this would not come again. And Mr. Scholter appreciated Ian's initiative. Without being told, Ian reorganized the hangars, placed wheel shocks in a neat line, and curled tie lines. He also dipped sticks into the underground fuel tanks to determine when fuel had to be ordered. He cleaned the training planes and removed candy wrappers and lunch bags that students left behind. On windy days, he ensured that one hangar door was always closed, to avoid a venturi effect on planes inside the hangar. At the end of August, Ian was rewarded for his good work. Mr. Scholter let him taxi planes, Piper Cubs first, then bigger planes with starters.

In winter, when flying was restricted, Ian helped with inventory. Scholter Aviation, as a dealer for Piper aircraft, had an extensive parts department. Customers flew in from Eastern Ohio, West Virginia, Central Pennsylvania, to buy parts. Ian recalled that it took three days to count rolls of aircraft fabric, engine and flight instruments, sideslip indicators, tachometers, compasses, gages, carburetors, magnetos, and spark plugs. Richard George taught Ian how to clean and gap the plugs, twenty to forty a day. Then there was the pile of aging airplane parts and scrap. By the second winter, Ian spent hours inspecting each piece of leftover scrap, then tagged it the best he could for disposal or retention. The disposable parts he loaded on a truck to be sold to a junkyard.

The reduced winter work schedule left Ian free time to socialize. The pay he earned meant he could go out with friends and see a movie. His mother, however, was still safeguarding his earnings. To receive money for an outing, Ian had to provide a carefully detailed accounting before she doled out the precise amount he requested.

As words got around that Ian was working at the airport,

he gained popularity. He had transferred to Butler High School, which had a higher academic rating than the local Penn Township School. Butler High was in a different tax base, which meant he had to pay a monthly 20-dollar-tuition. He learned later that the money, like the violin lessons, came from T.W. Phillips' trust fund. In his junior year he took a basic

High school meteorology class. Ian on the right, leaning over.

aviation class and impressed his teacher, Mr. Clawson, with his knowledge. Mr. Clawson had a pilot's license and taught about airplane parts and navigation. The class, Ian said, was the only one in which he received an A that year.

In May 1951, nearly two years after Ian's initial workday at the airfield, Mr. Scholter watched Ian taxi a Stinson to the hangar. As Ian climbed down from the plane, Scholter commented on Ian's good work habits and asked if he knew he could get flight lessons at a fifty percent discount. Ian had not been aware of that. He already knew the cost: $ 11.50 per hour in a Piper Cub with an instructor; $ 8.50 without an instructor, flying solo. Ian calculated that he would have to pay an instructor the full fee, but the plane would only be $4.25 an hour, and a total of $ 7.25 for a one-hour-lesson. Mr. Scholter said the cost could be deducted from his earnings. However, Ian needed a flight physical and a student pilot license, which required the approval of his parents. To fly a plane at sixteen seemed an unreachable goal. Mr. Scholter insisted Ian should try. Still, Ian was unsure. The cost was of concern. He said he had to think about it and ask his parents.

I have no doubt that Ken Scholter saw something in Ian that recalled his own youth, of a lad enamored with aviation. Their stories are similar. Ken was twelve in 1922 and on his bike when he noticed a small plane circling overhead. Curious about the plane's heading, Ken had chased it, pedaling all the way to Pittsburgh-McKeesport Airport, later renamed Bettis Field. He began working there as a gofer. He washed planes and learned how to be an airplane mechanic. Pilots nicknamed him "Monk," short for "Grease Monkey." Ken loaded the first bag of airmail to leave Pittsburgh and, whenever he could, hitched rides in airmail and civilian planes. After receiving his pilot license, he set an American record at a Detroit air show in 1931 for altitude flying to 17,540 feet in an Aeronca C-3 with a 36-horsepower, two-cylinder engine. His license for that show, (the *Federation Aeraunautique Internationale*) was signed by Orville Wright. Scholter went on to become a designated maintenance inspector and flight instructor. He taught in the Civil Pilot Training Program of the CAA (Civil Aviation Administration) and managed the Butler-Graham Airport for 35 years, which in 1991 was renamed K.W. Scholter Field in his honor.

On June 4th, 1951, with parental blessings, Ian had his first flight lessons in a Piper J-3.

Benjamin Brewster was Ian's flight instructor. Middle-aged, brown thinning hair, six feet tall but portly, Benjamin was

Above and below: *Ian's first flight logbook*.

not the epitome of good looks. His eyes were always hidden behind aviator Ray-Ban sunglasses. But Ian saw goodness in his smile and looked up to Mr. Brewster. Ian took to flying like an eaglet to air. Stalls and recovery, steep turns, crosswind and downwind landings, slow flight. These Ian performed after one demonstration, and without fear. Someone gave him a copy of the Civil Air Regulations to study. Ian passed the test on August 3rd, and soloed on August 6th, 1951, after only five hours of dual instruction. Ian would have to wait another year to receive his private license. By then he had enrolled in the Spartan School of Aeronautics.

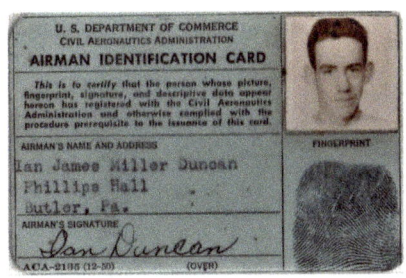

Ian's Temporary Student Pilot and solo certificates.

5

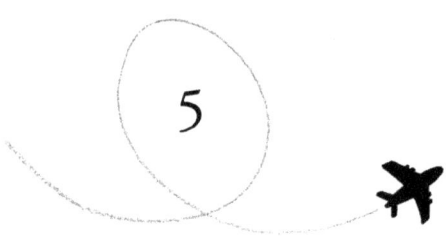

Besides flying, Ian had a passion for the outdoors. He was eleven when two of Mr. Phillips' groundkeepers, Ed and Frank Sheppeck, fostered Ian's interest in hunting. The brothers had known Ian since childhood and watched him grow up. Then they left to serve in the Second World War. In 1946, Ed and Frank returned and resumed their old jobs. Frank did not have children, and Ed was newly married. The men liked young Ian, knew his father was not a hunter, and offered to take Ian with them to hunt rabbits on the estate. An ecstatic Ian quickly learned basic hunting safety. Watch out, he was told. A rabbit could run out from anywhere, so immediately duck! Often, shots were fired above Ian's head. Whenever Frank or Ed killed two or more rabbits, they let Ian take one home to his mother. To Ian's delight, she prepared a hearty rabbit stew with onions, carrots, and potatoes.

At thirteen, Ian bought his first shotgun. His mother, after much hesitation and concern, doled out eighteen dollars from his caddy earnings. Shells were a nickel each, or twenty-five per box for $1.25. The gun, a Steven 16-gauge single shot, was stored under his parents' bed, and they determined when Ian could use it. There was no hunter's safety course.

Yet a tragedy two years later traumatized fifteen-year-old Ian and taught him the importance of gun safety. Roger Phillips and his wife Virginia had a three-year-old boy. One late afternoon in 1950, Roger took his young son to visit his grandfather in the mansion. The unsupervised child ventured into T. W. Phillips' bedroom, discovered a handgun in the bed stand, and shot himself in the head. Ian's father was summoned to rush the boy to a Pittsburgh hospital. A police escort did not make a difference. The three-year old was dead on arrival. The incident bothered Ian for a long time. He had known the little fellow, watched him play, and could not accept the tragedy of his death.

Except for the occasional pheasant, Ian shot rabbits and squirrels solely on the privacy of the estate, which did not require a license. During the winter of 1950/51, when Ian was almost sixteen, Frank took him deer hunting. By then Ian had been working two summers for Mr. Scholter and could afford to buy his own rifle, a Mossberg 30-30 with four shots and a clip. With Ed's help, Ian practiced on targets, bought a license, and shot his first doe just outside the Phillips' fence. Ed taught Ian how to field-dress and skin the animal. A butcher in town handled the rest.

Two of Ian's high school buddies, George Marshall and Ed Lutz, were also hunters. The following winter, the three set out in George's 1937 Ford Sedan to hunt in Elk County. Only George shot a deer. Excited over the successful hunt, they had ignored the distance to the main road. Ian recalled how they took turns dragging the carcass two miles back to the car, then bound the deer over the fender.

Unlike his friend George, Ian did not own a car. Only on rare occasions was he allowed to drive his father's car to a sporting event on Friday night or to eat at Butler's notorious Hot Dog Sandwich Shop. And because Ian was a tuition student at Butler High, he had to provide his own means of transport. No public transportation or school bus were available. His mother did not drive, his father could not chauffeur Ian and his sisters the eight miles back and forth to school, so they hitchhiked. Then in his junior year, Ian paid a weekly gas allowance to classmates for a ride.

One of them, Bob Minor, proposed an outing to Pittsburgh to attend a burlesque show where women undressed on stage. For several months, Bob and Ian plotted the trip. Would the females really take off their clothes? Ed and George, Ian's hunting buddies, wanted to go, too. The entry fee was $3.50, a small fortune, and the minimum age to enter was eighteen. They were sixteen! Nonetheless, one Saturday evening, the four of them headed in Bob's 1939 Chevrolet sedan to Pittsburgh for the ten o'clock show. They planned to lie about their ages and debated how much they would be able to see. Would their seats be close enough? Would the females undress completely? They never found out. The woman at the ticket booth demanded identification. Greatly disappointed, they drove home. Still, they did not abandon hope, decided to try again, and had better luck weeks later in Youngstown, Ohio.

Meanwhile, for local entertainment, the boys and girls of Butler High went to school dances at the town's armory. To cover the cost of electricity, each student paid 25 cents for admission. Ian's classmate, Ed Hickey, had formed a band and provided music for the sock hop, supervised by teachers who occasionally offered a short lesson in dance steps. Ian thought he was a poor dancer whose three feet got tangled up. Somehow, he must have learned. In later years, we enjoyed many hours on the dance floor, though Ian would not have made the cut on Dancing with the Stars! Yet Ian liked music. Throughout high school, he played the violin in the school's orchestra. Ian said he was no talented musician but recalls playing a pizzicato solo movement during a year-end performance.

Ian, front right.

Then, in his senior year a special opportunity arose. He had joined a promotional team to advertise a school play. What would be the best way to get the information to a large audience? Drop leaflets from an airplane all over Butler, Ian decided. He enlisted the help of Harry Fisher, a pilot from the Second World War. Harry owned a sawmill and the lumbering rights on seven acres of public land. He also owned a Monocoupe, a powerful little plane, ideal for aerobatic maneuvers. The previous summer, Ian had flown with Harry, who demonstrated barrel rolls, loops, lazy eights, the kind of flying an inexperienced student normally did not learn. Now, months later, Ian and Harry flew over Butler's main streets and dropped two thousand leaflets. The police, unhappy with the mess around town, filed a complaint with the school. Upset street cleaners called the mayor. Students were ordered to clean it up. But the play was a sold-out success.

"What about dating in high school?" I asked. Ian told me he was a bashful teenager and did not ask a girl out until he turned sixteen. Highly coveted private gatherings were rare, and it was an honor to make the list. Ian said two of his friends never got invited. His first invitation came in his junior year. A fellow violinist in the orchestra gave a party and asked Ian to come. That night, they played a popular kissing game. Seated on the floor in a circle, a player spun a bottle and, where it stopped spinning, that person had to be kissed. If the bottle pointed to a person of the same sex, the bottle was given another spin.

In his senior year, Ian fell in love. Joanne Knauer, a cheerleader and straight-A student, was petite, slim, and athletic. According to Ian she was pretty but no great beauty. In a 1952 yearbook photo, I see a serious-minded girl. Short brunette curls frame her heart-shaped face. Yet her eyes and mouth suggest a hidden sensuality. Ian had known Joanne for some time. They shared a homeroom, and she played clarinet in the school's orchestra. Now, the two met once a week to go to a movie or a dance. Apparently, Joanne was an excellent dancer. Any form of dance Ian knew, he says he learned from her. Both Joanne and Ian's parents discouraged steady dating. No doubt, unwanted pregnancy was a concern. Their young love would not turn serious until after high school graduation.

6

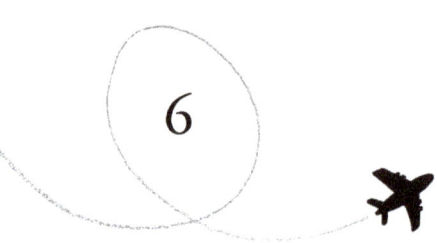

After his solo flight on August 6th, 1951, Ian kept working for Scholter Aviation and took instructions in a World War II Link Trainer, parked in Hangar One. With a hood and a full set of instruments, the trainer ran off an electric vacuum pump. A set of air-driven bellows made it pitch and roll. The trainer was cheaper to rent than an airplane. According to his flight logbook, Ian flew twice a week until school resumed, then only once a month.

One flight never left Ian's memory. A gusty northwesterly wind blew that day. The weather was so bad that Ben Brewster and Ken Scholter hesitated to let Ian take off. But Ian insisted. Sooner or later, he would have to handle flying in strong winds.

Link Trainer, originally used during World War II.

Eventually Mr. Scholter agreed to let him go and said, "We'll see what you're made of." The turbulence, Ian recalls, was awful: frightening and exciting at the same time. At 1500 feet (of altitude), the plane bounced left to right, up and down, and during approach, struggled against the strong headwind. Ben and Mr. Scholter were highly amused, as they later recounted, watching the aircraft swerve and bob to reach the runway. At a groundspeed of ten miles an hour, the plane was difficult to control. Ian recalls a triumphant thrill when the wheels finally touched the ground. As Ian descended from the plane, the two men noticed his disheveled look and laughed. Then they congratulated Ian for a job well done.

To be eligible for a private pilot license, the Federal Aviation Administration (FAA) required that a student log a minimum of 35 hours. In February 1952, Ian had flown only twelve. He was not sure how he could pay for the additional 23 hours. The cost seemed prohibitive. Ian knew his parents could not afford the expense. But his father thought there was a solution. He would take Ian to the Fidelity Trust Company in Butler and speak with Mitchel Uram, the trustee officer. Until then, Ian knew nothing about the money T. W. Phillips had allocated for his education. His parents had not mentioned it. But they had urged Ian to take college preparatory classes and told him that help might be available, if and when he were admitted to college. Today Ian understands why his parents did not speak about the trust. They felt large amounts of money could spoil a youngster's incentive to work and study. George and Isabella Duncan wanted their children to appreciate hard work and its reward.

For this reason, Ian did not know what to expect when he and his father entered the bank and were ushered into Mr. Uram's office. After the initial introduction and pleasantries, George Duncan asked Mr. Uram if the money allocated by Mr. Phillips for Ian's education could be used for flight training at the Butler-Graham airport. Mr. Uram pulled a document from a file cabinet, leafed through its pages for the appropriate part, then read out loud. In so many words, it said:

In the event that Ian James Millar Duncan, the said beneficiary, desires to attend college or some institution of higher learning and is unable to do so by reason of lack of funds, the said Trustee shall.... In short, the trust was solely for educational purpose. Money from the fund would be paid directly to a higher education establishment.

Ian could not make sense of the agreement's legal terminology. (I discovered a 2-page carbon-copy of the document in Ian's files.) Mr. Uram explained the purpose of T. W. Phillips' trust was for higher education, which would include the cost for a commercial license. Yet Mr. Uram suggested a more sophisticated training facility would be more appropriate than the local airport.

Ian was astounded. Even his father seemed happily surprised and asked about the current fund's value. Mr. Uram calculated the amount to be around $ 25,000, depending on the sale of stocks. Ian, after composing himself, asked if the fund also paid for room and board. Mr. Uram said both would be included. The news made Ian emotional, almost brought him to tears. He had scraped for nickels and dimes, worked at whatever was available, then suddenly been handed a pot of gold and could realize his dream.

The following day he gave the good news to Ben Brewster. There would be money to train for a commercial license. Mr. Brewster told Ian there were better places to pursue a career in flying than Scholter Aviation. He suggested Ian apply to the Spartan School of Aeronautics in Tulsa, Oklahoma. Ben Brewster was a graduate of the school, which had been founded in 1928 by W. G. Skelly, a man who envisioned a rise in air transportation and foresaw the need for skillful pilots and technicians. The school's training reputation attracted students from around the world, including various armed forces. Since 1942, J. Paul Getty had been Spartan's owner and expanded it to train TWA pilots, G.I Bill students, and after 1947, United States Air Force mechanics.

Ian applied immediately and was accepted for a class date in early July 1952.

7

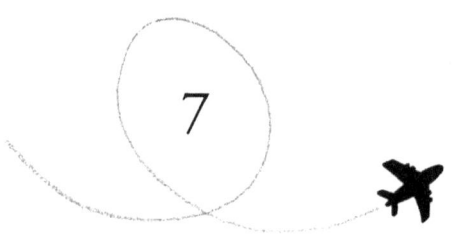

A photo from July 5th, 1952, at Pittsburgh airport, shows Ian's mother and sisters smiling, as if to commemorate a joyful occasion. Ian looks solemn, stands a foot apart, and appears ready to leave. What went through their minds? There must have been sadness. Never had Ian been away from Butler and his family. And this was to be his first ride on a commercial airliner, TWA to St. Louis, with a continuation on American Airlines to Tulsa. I asked Ian if he remembered the mood that morning. Was he stressed, sad, enthusiastic? He admitted to a degree of anguish. Yet an exciting future awaited him, and he was ready for it. At the departure gate, his sisters were emotional as they said

Ian with his sisters and mother at the Pittsburgh Airport, July 1952.

goodbye; and his mother barely managed to hold back tears. Only his father maintained a stoic composure. He urged Ian to do well and make the family proud.

Then Ian walked across the tarmac toward a TWA Constellation. Startled by the plane's size and its four engines, Ian wondered how one person could fly the airliner. He climbed the stairs and, once inside, glanced in the cockpit. Three uniformed men were busy at the controls. His question answered, he walked to the rear of the plane and settled in his assigned window seat in economy class. Would he one day fly a plane this size? The thought seemed unrealistic that morning.

Ian reminisced with me about the days before his departure. Ever since high school graduation a month earlier, time had accelerated. To save money, he had worked as many hours as possible. And in view of his pre-paid Spartan flight training, he had foregone all flying except for a short cross-country solo in a Piper Cruiser to Youngstown and back. Joanne and high school friends had been awestruck when Ian told them he was going to the Spartan School of Aeronautics. They wondered how he could afford a fancy flight school. After graduation, most of Ian's pals began work in local factories and farms. Ed joined the navy. Joanne became a full-time bank clerk. When asked monetary questions, Ian was vague. A kind of bank loan, he said, not forgetting that his parents had urged him not to reveal the source of the money.

I asked if he met with Mr. Phillips before his departure. Ian recalled being summoned to the mansion the day after high school graduation. Mr. Phillips congratulated Ian and gave him a ten-dollar-bill. He also expressed his pleasure that Ian would pursue higher education. But he did not mention money or a trust fund. Today, Ian agrees with me. At seventeen, he could not have fully understood the magnitude of Mr. Phillips' generosity.

After landing in St. Louis, Ian boarded a Convair-240 to Tulsa. During the hour and a half flight, he thought about the days ahead. Who would be his roommates? Would they be his age or older? (He soon learned that he was the youngest student on campus.) Ian tried to imagine what his teachers would be like. Would they be as encouraging as Ben Brewster and Mr. Scholter? Ben had assured Ian that he would meet good people, receive excellent training, and have fine weather for flying. Mr. Scholter had been enthusiastic and wished Ian well. Still, Ian worried about academics. Failure, he knew, was not an option. He had signed up for back-to-back courses and did not know how long he would be at Spartan. A year or longer? He had carefully packed a suitcase with summer and winter clothing. When the plane began its descent into Tulsa, Ian unfolded the letter of introduction from the school and re-read the information: Upon arrival, he should leave the terminal, cross the street, enter the Spartan building, and find Registration.

It was five in the afternoon when Ian entered the school. A registrar showed him around, pointed to the medical office, the scheduling department, gave him his class sessions, then guided Ian to the dining hall behind the dorms. He was handed a punch-card and the meal schedule: Breakfast 6:00 to 9:00, lunch 11:00 to 1:30, dinner 4:30 to 7:00. Whenever Ian went through the food line, a server would punch a hole for the appropriate meal. Once the card was full, a new one would be issued.

The barracks where Ian would live had two sections: a large military-style open dormitory with cots, and a second area of private rooms, each designed to accommodate four students. Bathrooms with showers were down the hall. There was a common day-room where students could meet, study, and read. Ian's trust money allowed for a private room. It was sparsely furnished with two bunks, a ceiling light, a table with a desk lamp, and four chairs. When he entered the room, none of his roommates had arrived. A set of sheets and towels was on each bed. Ian unpacked, placed his clothes in one of the four lockers, and went to the dining hall for dinner. There would be time later to make his bed. He stopped at a small store near the dining hall and bought a postcard to let his parents know of his safe arrival. On his way back to his room, he passed a long line by the coin-operated phone in the barracks' hallway. Ian remembered his father's words: "Do not call unless it's an emergency." The few times Ian made use of the phone, he called collect. His parents' number remained forever in his memory: Butler 2392.

The following morning a knock at the door and, "Wake up. Breakfast in fifteen minutes." In exchange for free meals, one student was assigned to get everyone out of bed. After breakfast, Ian started ground school, received aircraft manuals, and a sectional chart of aerial ground photos that covered a 100 mile radius. He had to become familiar with the terrain before his first flight on July 8th. From that day onward, and with few exceptions, Ian flew daily. His pilot logbook shows that on occasion he flew twice. Flight training and ground school alternated weekly between morning and afternoon. No free time for Labor Day and Thanksgiving. Classes were intense, with frequent written and oral tests in navigation, meteorology, aviation history, regulations, aircraft components, and maintenance. Ian said he was determined to excel. Fun and games were not on his mind.

Ian's school payments came directly from The Fidelity Trust Company. One check was for ground school and flight courses, another to the registrar for room and board, which included Ian's twenty-dollar weekly allowance. When Ian's account became due, the school handed him a bill to be mailed to his parents. They contacted Mr. Uram at Fidelity Trust, who sent the funds directly to the school. None of the money passed through Ian or his parents' hands. Ian's allowance covered laundry expenses. Most students had to do their own laundry, but each Monday Ian placed his in a white bag with his name on it. His clothes were returned on Thursdays, clean and ironed. Ian was not wanting and, being a cash student, the school treated him favorably. Yet his mother, he told me, mailed an occasional five dollar bill for extra spending money.

Two days after Ian's arrival, his roommates moved in. Philippe Reyes and Nelson Estrada came from Bogotá, Colombia, Saoud Salaam from Beirut, Lebanon. They were in Ian's flight program and had the same schedule. The four often ate and studied together. Although they spoke English, the two Colombians communicated in Spanish. Ian has retained some expressions, mostly swear words like *puta, mierda, maricon.* Saoud who spoke Arabic, French, and English, soon changed his name to Frank. "Why Frank?" I asked. Ian could not recall, only that it was easier to pronounce and remember. Ian was not a common name then. Annoyed at having to clarify his name repeatedly, Ian opted to use his second name. He said, "Call me Jim." From that time and throughout his working career, Ian became known as Jim Duncan.

Because the roommates were older, (Saoud/Frank the oldest at 22), the three subjected Ian to friendly teasing. "Poor Ian must stay in the dorm while we're off to a bar, to meet girls and drink beer." The place to go was a nearby Country Music Hall with a large dancefloor. Local girls went there unaccompanied. Luckily Ian had already developed a healthy sense of humor and was not offended. He liked his roommates. But going to a bar had to wait until his eighteenth birthday in January. In late August, Philippe and Nelson moved to a different room to be with their South American friends. A new roommate, Richard Davis, arrived. He had driven his brand new, baby blue Lincoln convertible from Charlottesville, Virginia. The next arrival was Rodney Castanah, a charming and good-looking native Hawaiian from Honolulu. Both were older than Ian. Rodney already had a private pilot license, which Ian earned on September 3rd, two months after arriving at Spartan.

Ian did not intermingle with other students but respected them, even a young man who suffered from dwarfism. The fellow was studying to become an airplane mechanic and worked part-time at a Boeing assembly plant for B-47 aircraft near the Tulsa airport. His small size was ideal for placing wires in wing structures. And because he used his arms as much as his legs to raise himself up, he had strong muscles. Sadly, some students ridiculed him, made comments about him needing a stool to reach the sink. The cruel remarks offended Ian, who empathized with the little guy. Then one day, the dwarf surprised everyone. Before anyone could stop him, he tackled the offender, sat on his chest, and pounded the fellow's face with his fists until others pulled him off. From that day onward, word got around the school: "Don't mess with the dwarf."

All students were allowed a two-week Christmas break. Richard, Ian's roommate, was traveling to Virginia by car and offered Ian a ride if he helped pay for gas. Jack Somerfield, a student from a small-town near Pittsburgh, joined them. The three left Tulsa early on December 21st, drove through the night, and arrived in Charlottesville the following morning. Richard dropped Ian and Jack at a gas station. From there they took a bus to Washington National airport, bought tickets to Pittsburgh on Capital Airlines. Ian called his father, who came to fetch him at Pittsburgh airport.

Once home, Ian used his father's car to visit friends, along with seeing Mr. Scholter and Ben Brewster. He also wanted to impress Joanne with his flying skills. During his absence, Ian had developed serious thoughts about her and proposed a steady, monogamous relationship. In a letter he had promised that she would be his first passenger. Ian fulfilled his pledge the morning of Christmas Eve. Undeterred by an outside temperature of 36 degrees, the two drove to Alameda field, a now forgotten single-grass strip, where Ian rented a Piper Coupe. He purposely did not take her to the Butler-Graham airport. He wanted to be alone with her and avoid silly comments from friends and workmates at Scholter Aviation. According to the weather Almanac, visibility was good, wind conditions a light breeze for the twenty-minute flight over Butler. A few days later, Joanne's parents invited Ian to dinner. Her father, a steel-mill worker, opposed his daughter's infatuation with Ian. Her mother adored him. Ian pledged his love for Joanne, said she would be the only one, and gave her his class ring as a token. Yet he hesitated to become intimate before his return from Spartan the following spring.

Ian's second passenger was George. After flying with Joanne in the morning, Ian drove home, picked up his father, and rented a Piper J-3 from Mr. Scholter. His mother had a fit when Ian told her she could not come because he would be unable to hoist her plump body into the plane. Apparently, she held that comment against Ian for a long time. To appease his mother for not taking her flying, he agreed to church on Christmas day. She insisted he wear a suit, tie, and proper shoes, not the aviator boots he had worn home. Ian was told to walk the aisle to the family pew and sit by his mother. Her church friends had to get a good look at her aviator son as she called him. Ian hated being put on display. "You know my mother," he quipped.

On December 28th, before returning to Tulsa, Ian gave his sisters a ride in a Stinson. When the plane took off, snow and ice covered the ground, and the temperature was 25 degrees. Ian recorded the flight time as one hour. Then on January 3rd, Ian's father drove him to Pittsburgh airport where he met Jack. The two flew to Washington National, met Richard in Charlottesville, and drove back to Tulsa. On January 8th, Ian passed the check ride for his commercial pilot diploma, which he could not hold legally until his 18th birthday nine days later.

Ian in 1952 with his mother, father, and Isobel.

The school's tight organization impressed Ian. Most of the instructors had flown in the Second World War. The training aircraft, Piper J-3s with sixty-five horse-power engines, were kept in optimum condition. Not once, with a student aboard, did an engine failure occur. Each morning, instructors flew the planes from Tulsa airport to Harvey Young Field, a grass strip ten miles away, where flight training took place. Bill Avery, the man in charge of scheduling and transportation, drove flight students in an eight-passenger van back and forth to Harvey Young. Two bus frames mounted on blocks served as a waiting area. If a student could not get back in time for lunch or dinner, Mr. Avery delivered a carry-out meal. At the end of the day, students and instructors flew the planes back to Tulsa on a set route. The J-3s were not equipped with radios. Prior to takeoff, the Tulsa tower assigned the landing runway by telephone and used standard light signals for clearance to land.

I asked Ian about specific flights. Had he encountered unexpected or unusual circumstances? He recalled a sticky situation on September 27th, three weeks after he received his private license. That day, he was to fly a Stinson on a cross-country flight to Waco, Texas. His roommate, Saoud, wanted to come along, which was against school regulations. Ian said Saoud was the instigator, which was more than likely true. Having met Saoud in later years, I came to know his persuasive smile and happy-go-lucky attitude. To avoid being seen together the morning of their adventure, Saoud got a ride to Riverside airport, a small airfield six miles south of Tulsa, where Ian would land and pick him up. From there, the two young daredevils took off. Who would ever know? Obviously, they did not consider the consequences if the school were to find out. They landed in Durant, Oklahoma, to refuel. As Ian was taxiing back to the runway, he discovered that one of the plane's two magnetos was inoperative, which meant an automatic flight grounding. An aircraft magneto is a small self-driven electrical generator that does not require an external electrical source. Each magneto uses permanent magnets and coils to fire the two spark plugs in the engine's cylinders. If one fails, the engine still runs but at lessened power. Federal Aviation Regulations require that both be in working order. The school sent a mechanic with a new magneto. That day Ian flew back to Tulsa. But Saoud had a three-hour bus ride to Spartan.

As it turned out, a few days later, Ian headed alone to Waco. In Oklahoma, surveyors and farmers had created straight north-south and east-west lines, comprised of roads, fields, and property divisions. The lines were of some help to pilots for visual confirmation of compass headings. Yet in 1951, the area south of Tulsa had few topographical clues like roads and towns to determine current positions. As per visual flight rules (VFR), Ian used dead reckoning prior to departure to calculate his expected arrival times at certain points on his flight path, then took readings along the way to determine how the wind was affecting his progress. Halfway to Waco, Ian was flying in a south-westerly direction and scanned the terrain below. Nothing but dirt and tumbleweed as far as his eyes could see. According to his chart, there should have been a town below. He circled around. No community in any direction. Panic set in. He was lost. A pilot's nightmare! He calculated about 40 minutes of remaining fuel and returned to his original heading. Still nothing below looked right. Even the NSEW tell-tale lines were invisible. How could he have become so disoriented? Minutes passed. He watched the gas gage, hoped for some recognizable site below. Finally, a town came into sight. Did it have a name? Ian remembered from navigation class that ninety percent of southwestern towns have a water tower with clearly visible names. He descended, circled around the tower, saw the name, and felt relief. When he became an instructor several months later, he remembered to tell his students about water towers.

Ian also recalled the day he flew a plane backwards. In ground school he had learned this was possible, depending on specific wind conditions. But could he accomplish the maneuver in flight? He waited for a windy day to make it happen, took off, climbed to 3000 feet, headed the plane in the direction of the wind, and practiced slow flight, forty to fifty miles per hour. The maneuver was tricky. The slower the plane, the harder it was to control, and the stick had to be moved further to the up/down, left/right positions. To his amusement, Ian noticed the plane was in fact backing up in reference to the ground. With a grin, Ian said the exercise would have been perilous over an extended period.

"Why," I asked. "You can't see what's behind you!" was Ian's smart reply.

That same day I amused myself by looking through Ian's logbook from that year. I noticed flights out of different airports, and other models of planes. Ian said that to get a broader knowledge of civil aircraft other than the ones operated by Spartan, he had rented Cessnas, Aerocoupes, Taylorcrafts, and Stearmans at various local airfields. Again, his trust fund paid the expense. On one such occasion, he went to Claremore to rent a farmer's Stearman byplane, used as a crop duster. The farmer, stunned by Ian's boyish looks, asked, "*You* wanna rent my plane?" He emphasized the word *you,* then said, "They turn'em out young these days." Ian climbed into the open cockpit, took off and, listening to the sound of the wind, partnered with the aircraft. Like many pilots before him, he felt the thrill of flying a Stearman biplane.

Ian finished flight school within eleven months and left before his roommates. He had passed the flight instructor exam on March 19th and received his instrument rating on May 29th. Shortly before he returned home, Mr. Scholter called Ian's parents. Ben Brewster had taken an instructor job at an airport closer to Pittsburgh. Would Ian be interested in taking his position? Ian's answer was in the affirmative.

As to Ian's initial room-mates, Philippe Reyes and Nelson Estrada returned to Colombia and ended up flying for Avianca, the Colombian flag carrier. Saoud, who had married Jeannie, a hostess and cashier at Tulsa's airport restaurant, moved with his new wife to Beirut and became a captain for Middle East Airlines. Later when Ian and I flew for Pan American with lay-overs in Beirut, we met up with Saoud. By then he had divorced Jeannie and remarried. As to Ian's other buddies, Rodney flew many years for Hawaiian airlines. And Richard Davis, after obtaining his commercial and instrument ratings, returned to Virginia where he became the chief flight instructor and general manager of the Gordonsville Airport.

Back in Butler, Mr. Phillips asked for a brief meeting to congratulate Ian and ask about his prospects. Ian said the training at Spartan qualified him to be a commercial pilot. Yet he hoped to gain more experience. He also mentioned his 1-A draft classification. Ian felt strongly that a military adventure soon awaited him.

8

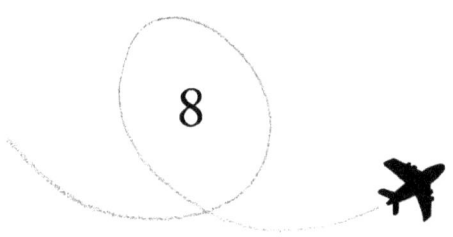

After returning home from Tulsa on May 30th in 1953, Ian led what he facetiously calls 'the exciting life of a flight instructor at a small-town airport'. Mr. Scholter guaranteed Ian a monthly base pay of 200 dollars (nearly 2,000 today) or three dollars an hour for basic flight and five for instrument training. Ian began instructing on June 2nd and logged 64 hours that month. The high demand continued through October, then decreased to 51 hours in December, before picking up again in March and April. Days off depended on weather or scheduled flight activity. During summer, when flight lessons were in high demand, Ian could easily exceed his 200-dollar basic salary and keep a reserve for the leaner winter schedule. Both he and Mr. Scholter knew the arrangement was temporary. The Korean War was ongoing, and Ian was sure to be drafted before year's end. He lived with his parents and used his father's car for transportation. Half his monthly paycheck went to his parents for room and board.

That summer, Ian and Joanne's love story deepened. Before then, their romance had been limited to petting and close contact on the dance floor. Ian recalls how shocked he felt when, during his Christmas break from Spartan, Joanne had taken his hand and placed it on one of her breasts. I asked Ian if marriage was ever discussed. Ian thinks she might have harbored hopes, but he does not recall a serious discussion about their future together. Ian wanted a military career and knew he had to be unmarried to enter the Aviation Flight Cadet program.

Because neither Joanne or Ian owned a car, his father's automobile became the one for going to a diner, drive-in movie, and for intimacy. Joanne was the first to suggest they have sex. A girlfriend having a sexual relationship told Joanne to try it, and not to worry about her virginity. Birth control pills would not be approved for another seven years. The young lovers depended on condoms. A retired policeman who owned a gas station near the airport, stocked them. Ian was careful to keep the condoms hidden. Not in the dresser drawer where his mother might rummage and see them. Joanne's and Ian's sex took place at night while parked on the Phillips' estate. One day, Ian's father, not knowing how to tackle the subject, remarked to Ian that a groundskeeper had found used rubbers in a field where sheep were grazing. "He hud seen yer car parked nearby." Without elaborating further, his father looked him straight in the eye and said, "Ian, mah lad, ye'r killing the sheep." Ian never parked on the estate again.

Although Ian prided himself on his accomplishments, as a new instructor he worried. Would people take a boyish-looking, lanky teenager, who had not yet shaved, seriously? His students were older, men without flying experience. Only Ben Brewster's former students, Ray White and Roger Whitesell, had reached an advanced level and hoped to become commercial airline pilots. One day, when a prospective newcomer saw Ian on a bench outside Scholter's business offices, he asked to be led to the person in charge of instruction. "You're looking at him," Ian said. The man chuckled and asked again where the instructor was. "You're still looking at him." Ian stood and led the man inside. At his desk, Ian explained the Scholter Aviation training program, the number of hours needed to obtain a private license, the cross-country and night flights. The customer was interested but wondered if older instructors were available. Ian mentioned two part-timers who worked weekends, which meant one or two lessons a week. With some reluctance, the man agreed to give Ian a try. Immediately Ian took him for a 'dollar plane ride', less than his usual rate of three dollars per hour. During the flight, Ian demonstrated basic flying technique, then let the man try the controls to see if he could hold a steady level. Two months later, the doubter had his private license and bought a plane from Mr. Scholter.

Ian described a typical flight lesson: He walked the student around the plane, explained the flight controls and cables, then climbed in the cockpit to discuss the instruments. This took about an hour. Next, he started the engine, which meant hand-cranking the propeller on the Piper J-3 and swinging it two to three times to get ignition. To maintain clear vision of the area ahead, the student was to taxi in S-turns to the end of the runway and, before take-off, do the obligatory magneto-check. Once airborne, the student flew a rectangular pattern at 800 feet of altitude, then prepared his glide path and turned on the carburetor heat before reducing the throttle to idle. (The throttle construction was such that ice could form internally even in warm weather.) Ian taught the student how to adjust the glide path and descent rate and, before landing, gradually raise the nose to arrive at the desired landing point. Once on the ground, he was to re-apply power and take off again. This way, the student could perform two to three landings within fifteen minutes. The difficulty for most students was deciding at which altitude to flare (landing pitch attitude), then to achieve a gentle glide to the runway and land on all three wheels simultaneously. Crosswinds made these landings more difficult. Before a student initiated his own stall, slow flight, or steep turns, Ian first demonstrated the procedures to make the student feel at ease.

There had been a young man, who after twenty hours of instruction, found himself lost on his first cross country solo from Butler to Erie. Ian recalled receiving a collect call mid-afternoon. The student had been disoriented and, rather than burning more fuel, landed safely in a farmer's field east of Erie. He wanted to know what to do. Ian said he should stay where he was and get the name of the nearest town, so Ian could find him. He would bring a second instructor to fly the plane out. But in Butler that day, no other instructor was available. Only Hans, the parts manager, a German immigrant with who had aviation experience, could accompany Ian. They took off in a high-powered Piper J-3 with a 90 hp engine, better suited for short field take-offs and landings. Once they had located the field and were on the ground, Ian let Hans take off ahead of him in the grounded plane, while he and the student followed in the high-powered one. By then too much time had elapsed. It would be dark before they reached Butler. The planes had no navigation lights, which required special batteries. (Piper

Cubs' batteries need to be installed prior to a night flight.) The two planes, flying illegally without navigation lights, were not spotted. Ian and Hans made it safely back. Or so they thought.

In recounting this story, Ian told me that once pilots had landed, they had to guard against the feeling that all was well. "A flight is not over until the plane is safely parked." Hans had failed to notice the taxiway marker light and ran over it. This caused minor damage to the propeller, which fortunately could be repaired at Scholter's shop. Instead of being angry with Hans, Mr. Scholter was grateful the student returned safely. But he insisted the young man's instruction continue before another cross-country flight was allowed!

Ian's only failure was a 50-year-old owner of a Taylorcraft. If Ian told him to taxi out, take off to the South, fly a left-hand rectangular pattern, then perform a touch and go landing, the man often went to the wrong runway. After fifteen hours, three times the norm, Ian let him fly solo. On the second or third landing, he flared too high, stalled, and hit the runway so hard that rubber bungies around the landing gear struts snapped. This caused one wing to tilt. But the student blamed Ian for what happened and said he should have been told the rubber could break. Fortunately, the man was unable to obtain a license, which made for safer skies, Ian quipped.

Scholter Aviation advertised passenger rides, and summer weekends brought a flurry of customers. Most people in 1953 had never sat in an airplane and were thrilled to see their homes from up high. For twenty-five dollars an hour, Ian could take three customers in the big Stinson Flying Station Wagon, an airplane otherwise used only for instrument flight training. For half the price, a single customer received a ride in the Piper J-3. Ian always asked passengers what they hoped to see and where they wanted to go. Would they like him to demonstrate a loop or a spin? But few were interested in such a thrill. The rides were bumpy enough, airsick bags standard equipment. Ian prepared female passengers with a 'special' pre-flight briefing. If they got scared, he said, they should feel free to hug him. It was meant as a joke. Ian received many hugs from elderly ladies, who were hesitant to look out the window and moved sufficiently left to get a hold of Ian's arm or neck. He lamented that the younger females did not take advantage of his offer.

In January 1954, a photographer called Scholter Aviation. He wanted to take aerial photos of Butler's industrial complexes and photograph terrain intended for future development. Mr. Scholter designated Ian as his pilot. Knowing the need for a clear blue sky, Ian studied the weather forecast and waited for a cold front to clear the atmosphere. The plane was going to be a three-seat Piper Super Cruiser with the back door removed to give the photographer a full view below. The day of the shooting, Ian and his passenger bundled up as if going on an Arctic expedition. Ian wore sheepskin pants and a jacket that had belonged to a World War II bomber pilot. For the photographer to get clear shots through the open rear door, Ian flew the plane in perpetual 360 degree right turns with the right wing down. They flew at an altitude of 500-1000 feet, and the drafty cold air meant the plane's heater could not maintain the cabin temperature from falling below freezing. After an hour or so, the photographer had more than one hundred pictures.

By the time they landed, he and Ian were shivering. Yet the mission was a success. Ian recalls that ten to fifteen photos later appeared in Butler's Chamber of Commerce magazine.

In retrospect, Ian reaffirms there was little glamor as an instructor pilot at a small-town airport. Still, there was some excitement that summer. On August 30th, 1953, a twin-engine de- Havilland Dove enroute from New York crashed near Grove City, forty miles north of Butler. Both the pilot and his girlfriend died. Scholter Aviation received a call from the Pennsylvania State Police to help with the investigation and remove the wreckage for salvage.

The morning after the accident, Mr. Scholter and Ian set out for what would be Ian's first-time to a gruesome crash site. What Ian saw stayed forever in his memory, of metal pieces scattered across a grass field. Although the human remains had been removed, there was visible body tissue on some of the plane's parts. How, Ian wondered, could an all-metal plane with decent-sized engines and propellers end up so obliterated? The aircraft must have stalled at great speed, hit the ground nose down, and summersaulted several times before it broke up. Mr. Scholter took photos to send to the insurer. Nothing of the plane was salvageable, and a car wrecking yard hauled away the debris. The cause of the accident remained undetermined. However, examination of the body parts that adhered to the plane's seats and cabin floor suggested one hypothesis: the pilot had put the plane on autopilot for a sexual interlude in the back seat.

Fortunately, the second accident that year had a comical element. State police called Mr. Scholter to tell him that a small plane had landed in a tree, one and a half miles east of Butler-Graham Airport. Mr. Scholter and Ian rushed to the site. The plane, a two-seater Aeronca Champion, destined for Butler-Graham, had run out of fuel. In attempting to deadstick a landing in a grass field, the pilot let the plane stall and plonked into a tall tree. There it remained, a hundred feet off the ground. The fire department's tallest ladder was not high enough to reach the plane. A young athletic fireman climbed the tree to the cockpit. He wrapped the pilot, a middle-aged student on a cross-country flight, into a bag-sling, which was lowered to the ground. The man was not hurt, though visibly shocked to have survived. Scholter's mechanics dismantled the plane and kept the salvageable parts.

In early 1954, the Butler County Airport Authority signed an agreement with a contractor to pave the east/west runway. The on-site supervisor, an affable guy, was a pilot in the Air National Guard out of Greater Pittsburgh Airport. During the Second World War, he had flown a P-51 Mustang and told Ian about high speed runs and aerobatic flying. This ignited Ian's desire to fly such a plane, and he asked what he had to do. The supervisor told him to watch for an advertisement in the *Butler Eagle* or the *Pittsburgh Press* that invited young men to join the Aviation Cadet Pilot Program. The ad would give the name of a recruiting office for preliminary testing and an interview. Ian hoped to see the ad before he was called for the draft, which was imminent. His mother's friend, who worked in the draft office, kept Ian up to date on the numbers.

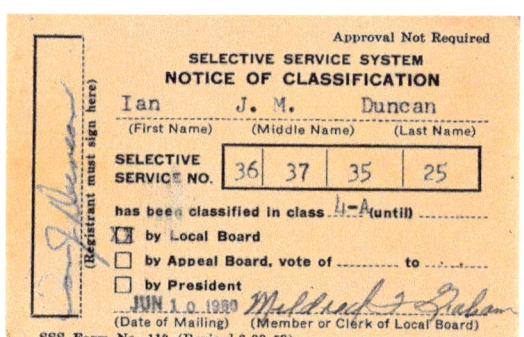

Ian's draft classification card.

Meanwhile Ian checked the papers daily for the ad, which finally appeared in early March. He called for an appointment, went for the interview, and met the prerequisites: a high school diploma, basic knowledge of English, good health, age eighteen, and single. Ian had them all.

The recruiter arranged for Ian to fly commercially to an Air Force Base in Utica, New York, for the Aviation Cadet Qualifying Exam, a three-day event that measured health, decision-making, mathematical skill, and leadership quality. The third day, Ian proved his hand and eye coordination, reflexes, and visual alertness on a psychomotor, a device that displayed small lights to measure flight control effects. Finally, he underwent an interview with a trained psychologist. Ian never broadcast that he already had a commercial and instructor license. Several persons, including the pilot for the Pittsburgh Air National Guard, had warned him not to mention his personal flying experience until his primary Air Force flight training. Two weeks after his evaluation in Utica, Ian was notified of his acceptance. The question was asked: How soon could he start pre-flight school? Immediately, he said. Ian received a starting date for May 20th, 1954, at Lackland Air Force Base, in San Antonio, Texas.

9

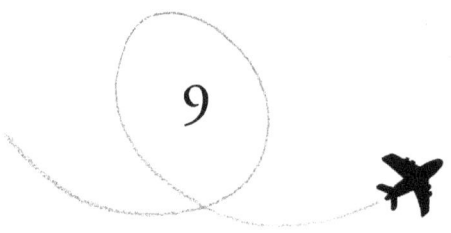

S an Antonio's heat and humidity shocked Ian that summer of 1954. The temperature at Lackland Air Force Base hovered between 80 and 100 degrees. The barracks were not air-conditioned, and before going to bed, Ian took a cold shower, then slept with only a sheet over him. Tired from a day of drills, marching, and classes in Air Force history, he fell asleep quickly. And thanks to years of walking and bike riding, Ian was in excellent shape. Despite the heat, he outran fellow cadets and was a good swimmer. He also excelled at jumping from a 75-foot tower and landing safely with an open parachute.

Convair XC-99.

Yet at Lackland that summer, Ian's biggest thrill was seeing a Convair XC-99 (the cargo version of the B-36 bomber), fly in and out of nearby Kelly Air Force Base. Five minutes before the plane was visible, Ian could hear its deep unmistakable drone. With its six pusher propellers, the double-decked plane, the largest piston-engine transport aircraft ever built, had the capacity to carry 100,000 pounds of cargo. At the time Ian could not imagine piloting such a behemoth, though later in life he flew the Boeing 747.

When basic cadet training ended late in August, Ian transferred to primary flight training at Malden Air Base in Missouri. The on-base living quarters reminded him of Spartan: four to a room, two bunkbeds, one shower, and a toilet shared with the adjoining room. Lights out at ten, rise and shine at five, a quick bathroom rotation, breakfast, and a full day's schedule. On August 31st, Major Polsgrove, the base chaplain, wrote Ian's parents these words: "Your son will receive the best character-building influences, and the military will instill in him the highest concept of leadership."

Ian had not disclosed his pilot qualifications and waited until his first flight. That day, before taking off in a Piper Pa-18, his instructor asked Ian if he had previous experience. Not wanting to divulge too much, Ian said he had been flying Piper Cubs and had a commercial license. "Let's see what you can do," the instructor said. Ian took off, demonstrated slow flight, stall, steep turns, spins, and recovery from them. The instructor referred Ian to the chief pilot. Again, Ian demonstrated what he knew. The chief pilot told Ian that he was more than qualified, that he would ask Air Force Training Command to waiver the primary full-flight instruction. A week later, Ian was summoned to see Major Hansen, the officer in charge. He told Ian that he would need to restart and fulfil the cadet primary flight curriculum because his prior flight experience was not in an aircraft with an engine over 450 hp. Ian tried hard to suppress his disappointment. Major Hansen wished him luck, hoped he would excel, and dismissed him. Once out of the office, Ian tried to reconcile his feelings. The news should not have surprised him. He had been warned not to count on his previous flight certificates. If the military paid the cost for a second training, he vowed to make the best of it, keep his mouth shut, hone his flying skills, and be the best in his class.

Although Ian did not have a choice then, I wondered how he felt today about the ruling. Had his flight training at Spartan been a waste of time? Ian said he was glad for the additional instruction, which deepened his skills in instrument and aerobatic flying with a radial engine. He was certain, however, if the United States had been at war, he would have been exempted.

For the following six months, Ian trained in a tandem-seat T-6 Texan with a big radial 600 hp Pratt & Whitney engine. It was the only plane he ever flew while wearing a full parachute. The T-6 was one of the best military flight trainers ever built and, for decades, facilitated flight instruction for thousands of pilots around the world. During the Second World War, a majority of allied forces trained in the T-6. Plus, the United States Air Force (USAF) used it as a spotter in the Korean War. Ian liked flying this plane because of its aerobatics capability. He could practice loops, barrel, aileron, and snap rolls, experiencing negative and positive G-forces, the kind of maneuvers he was most deficient in. To this day, he believes that all student pilots should fly a plane with a high-powered radial engine and a conventional landing gear (two wheels under each wing, one under the tail) to improve their flying techniques.

Top: *Tandem-seat T-6.* Above: *Ian in a T-6 at Malden.*

In October 1954, Ian's flight commander, in a letter to his parents, stated the following: "Your son is a well-balanced, clean, intelligent young man, one you can be proud of."

That fall in Malden, Ian bought his first car, a six-year-old Chevrolet Coupe that cost 400 dollars, four times his monthly cadet pay. To help with the expense, his mother agreed to take money from Ian's saving account. Having a car in Malden, surrounded as it was by farmland, raised Ian's popularity. Small towns and communities were miles apart. Five young men could squeeze in the Chevy for an evening at a drive-in movie or a bar. And weeks later, Ian drove home to Butler for Christmas and a happy family reunion. Both sisters, Helen and Isobel, were home from their respective colleges. Helen, Ian's older sister had become engaged to Robert Armstrong, a doctoral candidate at Ohio State. They married the following spring.

Helen, Ian, and Iz in front of the 1954 Chevrolet Bel Air.

While on Christmas break, Ian's father suggested that the old Chevy Coupe be traded for a newer model. Ian's saving account helped to pay for a 1954 two-door, red and white Chevy Bel Air. Ian's pride and joy! "A real beauty," he recalls with a smile.

As if the car were not flamboyant enough, Ian attached a metal plaque to the front license plate, advertising that he flew for Scholter Aviation. The plaque, a gift from Mr. Scholter the day Ian soloed, became a valued keepsake.

Left: *Scholter Aviation license plate plaque.*

Ian paraded the car through town. His friends at Scholter admired its beauty, Isobel's girlfriends hoped for a ride, old Butler High buddies were in awe. But not Joanne. After Ian joined the Aviation Cadet program, their love affair dissipated. He does not recall their last conversation or letter, only that the writing stopped. Perhaps Joanne recognized her limited chance of a future with Ian. She soon dated someone else but kept Ian's class ring. He did not dare to ask for its return.

Back in Malden the winter of 1955, a sad event occurred. Robert Westphal, a cadet from Kenosha, Wisconsin, along with his instructor, died in a plane crash. Wes, as he was known to his friends, had previously served as a flight engineer on the H-19 helicopter but hoped to become a commander on that aircraft. Ian liked Wes, had tutored him occasionally. Afraid of appearing stupid, Wes preferred to ask Ian for help, instead of his instructor. Ian taught Wes the importance of maintaining altitude during steep turns; and he warned about loss of power in relation to air speed, a dangerous scenario from which a pilot might not recover. As to a crosswind landing, Ian verbally described lowering the wing into a crosswind and landing on one wheel to offset the plane's tendency to weathervane. Wes was grateful for Ian's help. One day he mentioned his wristwatch, said it moved ahead at a fair speed, and needed to be reset several times within a 24-hour period. Two days later Wes was dead. An eerie coincidence, Ian said. Ever since, he has believed a fast watch needs to be thrown away.

That wintry day in 1955, Wes's accident occurred after the noon break. The warm lunchroom, a full stomach, the earlier five a.m. wake-up: all signals for the brain to relax, the body to seek sleep. 'Beware of the post-lunch hour' was a saying among cadets. No sooner had Wes taken off, than his instructor gave him a simulated engine failure. In the T-6, this required an immediate nose down to maintain air speed and select a forced landing site straight ahead. At gliding speed, the T-6 tended to snap roll in turns. Ian assumed the instructor had been slow to react, because Wes ended up in a double spin directly into the ground. In the briefing room, soon after the accident, Ian could not hold back tears. Oddie Shinault, Ian's flight instructor, urged him to get up. "Let's you and I go flying." Oddie made the take-off, then turned the plane over to Ian.

"You're a military pilot. You're going to face events more serious than this one. Remember you're a great aviator, and you will teach students to avoid such mistakes."

A memorial service for Robert Westphal was held February 4th, 1955. I discovered the program in Ian's memorabilia files.

Malden cadets craved females. Not until August 31st, 1955, when they became commissioned officers and received their wings, could they marry. To raise the cadets' morale on Friday and Saturday nights, the base brought in busloads of Missouri farm girls from as far away as 70 miles. The young women had to be eighteen, though Ian knew of younger ones being admitted. There was no I.D. check. And local mothers apparently encouraged the outings with the hope their daughters might marry an officer. A band or a DJ provided music. Drinks were fifteen cents. Since the girls outnumbered the men, the young cadets had a wide choice from the dating "buffet," as Ian called it. With a mischievous grin he mused that some unattractive officers ended up marrying good-looking girls. And when Ian became an upper-class cadet in early 1955, he made full use of his free time, known in the military as Open Post. He could come and go as he wished. But only as long as he was back on base by 11:00 p.m. In February, six weeks before he was to graduate, he met Tammy, a local girl, who with two of her friends attended the Friday night function. Tammy was cute, petite, lively. She and Ian flirted and danced, her arms stretched high to reach around his neck. Ian was smitten and asked where she lived, which turned out to be with her parents on a farm in

Kennett, 25 miles south of Malden. It was close to ten o'clock when Ian suggested he drive her home. During the drive, Tammy moved progressively closer. Had it been possible, Ian told me, she would have sat in his lap. When he felt her hand touch his thigh, he knew he was in trouble. Even a country boy from Butler knew this girl had more than kissing in mind. When they reached her parents' house, she urged Ian to stop short of the driveway and park. The front seat, too restrictive for sex, led to a passionate encounter on the backseat. Ian, horny and excited by Tammy's removal of her panties, could not resist. He lost track of time. His foot accidently hit a switch on the forward armrest, which turned on the overhead light, but this did not startle Ian enough to stop the act. When he came to his senses, he knew that he would arrive late on base.

It was 11:05 when Ian entered his room. His roommates, all three of them, were wide awake, staring at him like buzzards about to attack prey. "You're late!" Ian recalled their condemning voices but said he had no excuse. And rather than put them on the line, he offered to write his own 'gig' slip and take it to the commander the following morning. (A gig slip refers to a violation of a cadet's rule of conduct.)

Early on Monday Ian received a note that told him to report to Major Hansen's office. "Aviation Cadet Duncan reporting as ordered, Sir!" Ian noticed his training folder on the major's desk. "At ease, Cadet Duncan. Take a seat."

Major Hansen could not comprehend Ian's demerit slip. Why was an intelligent cadet knowingly late? Hansen knew that Ian was the top of his class and led lower ranking cadets in

AVIATION CADET HONOR CODE

Article 1: An Aviation Cadet will not knowingly make any false statement, written or verbal, while acting in any capacity, official or otherwise, or in any situation reflecting on the Aviation Cadet Corps or the Air Force.

Article 2: An Aviation Cadet will not take or receive the property of another person, or persons, under any conditions, without specific authority of that person or persons.

Article 3: An Aviation Cadet will not impart or receive any unauthorized assistance, either outside or inside the classroom or places of instruction, which would tend to give any Aviation Cadet unfair advantage.

Article 4: An Aviation Cadet will not quibble, use evasive statements, or technicalities in order to shield guilt or defeat the ends of justice.

Article 5: An Aviation Cadet will report any violation of honor by another Aviation Cadet of which he is witness or has unquestionable knowledge.

Article 6: An Aviation Cadet will not commit any act of intentional dishonesty which will reflect in any way on the honor and integrity of the Aviation Cadet Corps and the Air Force.

Above: *(Officer Code and Cadet Honor Code from brochure, "Aviation Cadet Knowledge," Preflight Training School, Lackland AFB TX)*

operations and training. "What's your wild excuse? A flat tire? Drunk?" Ian said he had no excuse. The major insisted that he give an explanation for what happened. Bound by the Cadet Honor Code, Ian told the truth.

"Cadet Duncan, there are two things that always get men in trouble. Drinking and women." He then told Ian what was going to happen. He would receive twelve demerit points, which meant six penalty marching tours and loss of 24 hours free time. Yet because Ian was six weeks short of graduation, his penalty would be deferred to his next assignment at Vance Air Force Base in Enid, Oklahoma. "Dismissed. Don't screw up again!" Pleased with the major's gallant offer, Ian left the office. This unpredictable outcome astounded his roommates. Ian ended up the outstanding cadet of his class. At the graduation ceremony on March 30th, 1955, Major Hansen, with a wink and a smile, handed Ian the top of the class trophy.

Major Hanson handing Ian the class trophy.

Forty-four years later, in 1999, Ian and I visited Malden as part of our North American journey in a Marathon motorhome. That October day we left our 'bus' in West Memphis, Arkansas, and drove the tow car, a Jeep Grand Cherokee, north on a nearly straight road, past fields and farmland and hawks on powerlines. During our monotonous two-hour drive, Ian reminisced about events from his cadet days, stories of flight, the military discipline, and young Missouri girls. He talked about Tammy and his demerit points. After his graduation from primary flight training and before driving to Butler for a few days leave, he wanted to see her again and rented a motel room for a night. He also stopped in Malden on his return, before driving to Enid. When Ian received his wings and became a commissioned officer that August, Tammy came to the ceremony. Ian's parents and sister Isobel, who also attended, worried he would marry her. But after moving on, Ian's interest dwindled. He said he did not want to be tied down like some of his cadet friends, whose girlfriends were waiting at the gate to get married. I did not need to remind Ian that within two years he had broken his pledge to remain single and married his first wife.

That fall in 1999, I saw an enormous flag at the entry of Malden Air Base. But the buildings were deserted. As we walked around, Ian pointed to the old tower, the housing, and spoke about fellow cadets. My thoughts that day went to the farm girls who dreamed of a little glitz outside country life. I asked Ian how many had held on to their charming prince? Ian said some might have tricked an officer and become pregnant to tie the knot. He assumed that the majority never left their Missouri homesteads. I have since learned that, in 2002, the base became a museum: The Malden Army Airfield Preservation.

In April 1955, when Ian arrived at Vance Air Base for advanced training, he immediately began serving the demerit penalty. Wearing a full uniform, including white gloves, he marched three consecutive Saturdays and Sundays, one hour at a time, on the base's tour ramp, a broad avenue. And for two more weekends, he was not permitted off base. The conditions that summer were hot and windy, typical of the Oklahoma dustbowl. Because cadet's rooms were not air-conditioned, windows had to be left open for air circulation, which meant Ian spent hours removing gritty dust. Tornados were prevalent, too. But Vance had a sophisticated warning system. On May 25th, 1955, a deadly category-five tornado destroyed the small town of Blackwell, 50 miles northeast. The news reported that twenty people perished and more than 400 homes were swept away. In the aftermath, news helicopters and emergency crews prevented anyone from the base to fly over the area. When Ian eventually did, the destruction impacted him gravely. Never before had he witnessed to such devastation.

Ian's aeronautical progression at Vance Air Base was a historic step in his aviation career. Because his goal was to work for an airline, he chose multi-engine flight training in the B-25, the aircraft used for the first raid on Tokyo in April 1942.

North American B-25 Mitchell.

The B-25 students at Vance flew a radius of 75 miles around Enid. Instructors were officers who had graduated within the past year. If he was not at the controls, Ian sat in the plane's nose turret, spotting traffic. Fifty B-25s could be airborne at the same time. The only overnight cross-country mission Ian flew was to Langley Field in Hampton, Virginia. This was unusual, as the military rarely allowed the expense of an overnight trip. "Why Langley?" I asked. Ian said his instructor had not been to Virginia and wanted to see the Chesapeake Bay. Elmer Faucet, Ian's roommate, was the other cadet on that flight. They stopped in Nashville to refuel and reached the Appalachian Mountains at night. By then weather conditions had deteriorated. Flashes of lightning put his instructor on edge. What if they lost an engine? Could they maintain altitude, avoid crashing into a mountain? They checked their charts for alternate airports. Fortunately, the engines prevailed, and they landed safely at Langley. Ian explained that an engine failure on the B-25 was a constant concern. Nowadays, 65 years later, he can recite from memory the emergency checklist for engine shut-down in-flight:

> ☐ Check ignition switches
>
> ☐ Check fuel shut-off valves
>
> ☐ Move mixture control to 'full rich'
>
> ☐ Turn on booster pumps
>
> ☐ Throttle back
>
> ☐ Feather propeller
>
> ☐ Fuel mixture 'idle cut-off'

Above: *Emergency Checklist*

By mid-July, Ian was eagerly anticipating graduation and his next assignment, which was awarded in order of class standing. Cadets were judged in compliance with Air Force rules and regulations, leadership qualities, respect toward fellow classmates, and airmanship. Being the outstanding cadet of his class, Ian hoped for his first choice, which was to fly the C-54, a four-engine transport plane, or the SA-16 Albatross, an amphibious plane for sea rescue. Unfortunately, neither was offered. His only choice was the C-119 out of Randolph Air Base near San Antonio. In early August, Ian had a fitting for his new Air Force uniform. His parents received a formal invitation to attend the ceremony on August 30th. Mr. Phillips congratulated Ian in a letter.

**HEADQUARTERS
FLYING TRAINING AIR FORCE**
OFFICE OF THE COMMANDER
WACO, TEXAS

31 August 1955

SUBJECT: Distinguished Graduate, United States Air Force Pilot Training

TO: Second Lieutenant Ian J. M. Duncan, AO3057662
      Class 55-U, Vance Air Force Base, Oklahoma

THE SECRETARY OF THE AIR FORCE HAS AUTHORIZED ME TO INFORM YOU THAT YOU ARE HEREBY DESIGNATED A DISTINGUISHED GRADUATE OF UNITED STATES AIR FORCE PILOT TRAINING.

DURING THE COURSE OF YOUR TRAINING, YOU HAVE DEMONSTRATED THAT YOU POSSESS TO AN UNUSUAL DEGREE THE ABILITY, INITIATIVE, AND OTHER LEADERSHIP QUALITIES SO ESSENTIAL TO SUCCESSFUL PERFORMANCE OF DUTY AS AN AIR FORCE OFFICER. YOU ARE DESERVING OF THE HIGHEST PRAISE.

IF YOU DESIRE TO MAKE A CAREER OF THE AIR FORCE, YOU WILL BE AFFORDED SPECIAL CONSIDERATION FOR REGULAR APPOINTMENT. A COPY OF THIS CORRESPONDENCE SHOULD BE ATTACHED TO YOUR APPLICATION WHENEVER YOU DO MEET EXISTING ELIGIBILITY CRITERIA AND APPLY FOR REGULAR APPOINTMENT.

CONGRATULATIONS ON YOUR OUTSTANDING ACHIEVEMENT.

G. P. Disosway

G. P. DISOSWAY
MAJOR GENERAL, USAF
COMMANDER

The graduation took place in a large indoor theater on base with the wing commander, who handed each graduate his wings. There was no trophy this time to honor Ian as the top cadet of his class. Instead, the three-star general in charge of Air Training Command presented Ian with a letter that stated his distinguished graduate award. This meant that, a year later, upon application, he would receive a regular officer commission, a big compliment, which put Ian in the category of a West Point or Naval Academy graduate. (The Air Force Academy was in its infancy, its first cadet class in 1955.) Unlike reserve commissioned airmen, who went into the Air Force Reserve, Ian as a regular was guaranteed twenty years of service, full retirement, and a pay increase: 500 dollars a month, a big step from his previous pay as a cadet. To my surprise Ian recited from memory his regular commission officer I.D. number: 48207A

When Ian returned home for Christmas 1955, Mr. Phillips was 81 and too gravely ill for visitors. Their final meeting had taken place earlier that year after Ian's Malden graduation. That day in April, Mr. Phillips had welcomed Ian to his study and greeted him with a warm handshake. They sat across from each other, with Mr. Phillips in his high-back armchair behind the desk. A half-smoked cigar emitted a sweet aroma from an ashtray. Ian briefly scanned the volumes of books and commemorative plaques that lined the walls. Mr. Phillips complimented Ian, said he was proud of him, and asked about his future plans. Ian said he hoped to fly multi-engine planes and eventually be an airline captain. The conversation turned to current events. Mr. Phillips spoke in a deliberate voice and was a quick thinker. Ian recalls their discussion about the ongoing Suez Canal oil crisis, and the struggle between Arab nationalists and the two remaining imperial powers in the region, Britain and France. Mr. Phillips asked what Ian knew about American military tactics in North Africa. Ian did not have an answer that day, could not have foreseen that within a year he would be flying Strategic Air Command tankers to Sidi-Slimane and Ben Guerir, U.S. air bases in Morocco.

**HEADQUARTERS
FLYING TRAINING AIR FORCE**
OFFICE OF THE COMMANDER
WACO, TEXAS

31 August 1955

SUBJECT: Distinguished Graduate, United States Air Force Pilot Training

TO: Second Lieutenant Ian J. M. Duncan, AO3057662
Class 55-U, Vance Air Force Base, Oklahoma

THE SECRETARY OF THE AIR FORCE HAS AUTHORIZED ME TO INFORM YOU THAT YOU ARE HEREBY DESIGNATED A DISTINGUISHED GRADUATE OF UNITED STATES AIR FORCE PILOT TRAINING.

DURING THE COURSE OF YOUR TRAINING, YOU HAVE DEMONSTRATED THAT YOU POSSESS TO AN UNUSUAL DEGREE THE ABILITY, INITIATIVE, AND OTHER LEADERSHIP QUALITIES SO ESSENTIAL TO SUCCESSFUL PERFORMANCE OF DUTY AS AN AIR FORCE OFFICER. YOU ARE DESERVING OF THE HIGHEST PRAISE.

IF YOU DESIRE TO MAKE A CAREER OF THE AIR FORCE, YOU WILL BE AFFORDED SPECIAL CONSIDERATION FOR REGULAR APPOINTMENT. A COPY OF THIS CORRESPONDENCE SHOULD BE ATTACHED TO YOUR APPLICATION WHENEVER YOU DO MEET EXISTING ELIGIBILITY CRITERIA AND APPLY FOR REGULAR APPOINTMENT.

CONGRATULATIONS ON YOUR OUTSTANDING ACHIEVEMENT.

G. P. DISOSWAY
MAJOR GENERAL, USAF
COMMANDER

Above: *Distinguished Graduate letter.* Right: *Second Lieutenant Ian Duncan.*

On January 2nd, 1956, Thomas Wharton Phillips Jr. died. Ian often spoke to me about his benefactor. Although linked only through his father, who was Mr. Phillips' chauffeur, Ian found a grandfatherly figure, a man who was always considerate and respectful toward him. Mr. Phillips showed a genuine interest in Ian and his sisters, was complimentary toward them, and seemed delighted that his personal investment in their education was fruitful. By the time of Mr. Phillips' death, Helen had earned a master's degree from Ohio State University; Isobel was working on a master's degree in nursing. And Ian was an Air Force lieutenant, soon to fly the KC-97. Mr. Phillips' own sons, who had been given every opportunity

Thomas Wharton Phillips Jr.

to achieve, were according to Ian's parents, somewhat spoiled and a disappointment to their father.

Below is Ian's tribute:

"My respect for Mr. Phillips went way beyond an average allegiance. He was my savior, and I paid homage to him with every successful event in later life. I recognized that very few young people were afforded the opportunity I had. And for that Mr. Phillips will always have my gratitude, admiration, and affection."

10

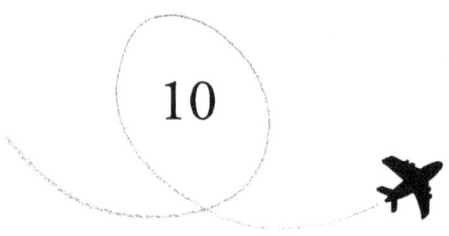

In early December 1955, Ian arrived at MacDill Air Force Base in Tampa. Would he join the bombardment or the air refueling squadron? He had not yet decided. His previous assignment after graduation at Vance on August 30th, had been Randolph Air Base, Texas, where he completed training in the C-119, the Flying Boxcar, so named for its box-shaped interior.

Ian had chosen the two-engine transport plane for a reason. It was designed to carry cargo, personnel, litter patients, and paratroopers. Ian hoped to quickly build flight hours and avoid

Fairchild C-119.

Strategic Air Command (SAC), where he estimated no more than 30 hours a month of flying. But his plan fell apart mid-October when the Air Force withdrew all C-119 assignments and offered only SAC bases. Why the military continued to train pilots in the C-119, when no slots were available, remains a mystery. Ian said he did not ask questions, enjoyed the flying experience, once again graduated top of his class, and was awarded his first choice: MacDill Air Force Base. Why MacDill? Florida's climate attracted him. Most of the SAC's bases were in the northern part of the United States.

During that era, the USAF's Strategic Air Command had built a global network of some seventy bases as far away as Greenland and North Africa. All were within striking distance of the Soviet Union, the primary nuclear threat to the United States at the time. And SAC was the biggest command, with approximately 270,000 personnel, 800 tankers, 2000 bombers, and some 3,000 aerial refueling missions per week. Most important was the combat radius, the maximum distance a plane could fly with a bomb load and return to base. MacDill Air Force Base had SAC's first operational B-47 jet bomber wing, followed by the 306th air refueling squadron in 1954. KC-97 Stratotankers refueled bombers on a perpetual basis, often in mid-ocean, which allowed them to fly three times their normal radius.

Ian's choices at MacDill were to fly the KC-97 Stratotanker, a four-engine, radial-piston-powered aircraft, or the B-47, a six-engine, turbojet-powered long-range strategic bomber. Both had their advantages, Ian told me. In later years, I had observed

Ian fly the tanker but could not recall the B-47. Ian reminded me that I had seen it on our travels to Florida, as the plane was highly visible from Interstate 95 in Georgia. And once we saw a B-47 on display at the Museum of Flight in Seattle. Still, I could not picture the plane, searched on-line, and found a photo of a B-47 taking off. The image made me speculate on the excitement of being at the controls of such a powerful aircraft. I asked Ian if he had been itching to get inside its cockpit. "Damn right," he said with a grin. By comparison, I thought the KC-97 with its massive head like a muskox, resembled the

Above: *Boeing KC-97 Stratotanker*. Below: *Boeing B-47 Stratojet.*

husky animal. Ian did not appreciate the comparison, but he agreed the plane did not project the B-47's charismatic appeal.

The main reason Ian did not favor the B-47 was being stuck for years in the backseat, which meant little actual hands-on flying time. At the officer's club, he heard B-47 backseat pilots complain of not getting enough take-offs and landings. Their commanders, Ian learned, were Second World War veterans, recalled for duty during the SAC build-up. They had little confidence in flying the plane and preferred not to cede control to their backseat pilots. And accidents happened frequently. On December 19th, 1955, Ian witnessed two B-47s collide over Tampa Bay. The two planes had been practicing take-offs and landings at MacDill. One of them had an unsafe landing gear indicator, and its commander asked for the second plane to approach and visually confirm from below that the gear was down and locked. Both aircraft were flying at a speed of 200 m/h, when turbulent airflow caused the lower B-47 to rise and collide with the one above. Locked together, both rolled down in a ball of flames. Four crewmembers died in the accident.

As to the KC-97, Ian would fly the right seat, which guaranteed more hands-on flying and an earlier chance to be in command. With some reluctance, Ian resigned himself to a career as a tanker pilot. He filled out pages of documents for a top security clearance, listed references to vouch for his trustworthiness, then presented the required paperwork to the chief personnel NCO, Master Sergeant Wilson. On a previous visit, Wilson had taken notice of Ian's home address, Phillips Hall, and asked if he was related to the Phillips. The question had stunned Ian. That guy knew the Phillips in Butler? Ian told Wilson he had grown up on the estate, that his father was Mr. Phillips' chauffeur. When asked how he knew the family, Wilson said he was a close friend of T.W. Phillips' oldest son, Thomas Wharton Phillips, the third.

In the personnel office a few days later, Wilson scanned Ian's folder and asked if he had made up his mind, warning him that, once on paper, the decision could not be reversed. "What plane it is going to be?" Ian told him the KC-97. Before Ian left the office, Wilson offered his continuous support and help with personal benefits and future assignments. "Remember," Wilson said, "I'm a friend of the Phillips." Ian told Wilson to give Tom his regards. (Nine years later, in 1964, Thomas Wharton Phillips III, died in Florida at the age of 47.)

Ian soon moved off base. A notice at the officer's club advertised a room to let. Two navigators were looking for a roommate to occupy a small addition to their two-bedroom house. Ian moved in, bought a bed, chair, and cheap wardrobe. A fan on top of a grapefruit crate created air circulation.

Two weeks short of his 21st birthday, Ian settled into the 306th air refueling squadron. He began his technical check-out of the KC-97's hydraulic and electrical systems, its pressurization and flight controls. He took classes in celestial, radar, and radio navigation, and observed seven night and day refueling missions. And he had to complete the mandatory winter survival training. Given its global operating environment, SAC trained all combat crews and personnel in how to survive remote, unfriendly terrain, how to evade capture, and how to escape.

In mid-February 1956, Ian and four members of a KC-97 crew, flew commercially to Reno, Nevada, and reported to Stead Air Force Base in the foothills of the Sierra Nevada. Keith, introverted yet professional, was the other pilot besides Ian. Louis and Art were navigators. Art, who was Jewish, loved to tell funny anecdotes. There was 40-year-old Norman, the boom operator and oldest of the group, who proved to be a hard worker. Each man carried a large greyish green canvas bag with two pairs of heavy woolen socks, long underwear, two blaze orange winter flight suits, full-flap headgear, fur-lined gloves, lace-up jump boots, and a face mask.

After two weeks of classes in ground navigation, evasion of captors, and nourishment in the wild, the five crewmembers left the base, dressed as if they had just vacated the KC-97's cockpit. Their equipment included a parachute with cords, snowshoes, and ski poles. In addition, they dragged a sled with two sleeping bags per man, a first aid kit, a 22-caliber rifle with ammunition, and emergency food. The rations included tins of beans, spam, tuna, onions, cabbage, and a small amount of water. A truck drove the team deep into the Sierra Nevada Mountains. The crew had seven days to find their way back to base via several checkpoints. A survival technician accompanied them to monitor their progress from afar, without intervening. Attitude was primary. Failure was not an option. Complainers and slackers were helicoptered out and had to leave SAC.

Each day, the crew trekked through snow, monitoring their whereabouts with the help of a sextant and a terrain chart, with a mission to reach their next checkpoint by dusk.

Above left: *Slow-going in snowshoes – about one mile an hour.* Above right: *Improvised parchute tents.* Bottom: *One member of the survival team spotted a porcupine up a tall pine tree. It didn't take long for it to make its way into Porcupine Stew.*

They took turns dragging the sled on a one-hour rotation. Depending on snow conditions, they advanced little more than a mile per hour. Ian recalls his snowshoes slamming up and down, regardless of how tight he fastened the leather thongs. Several times the shoe came undone. His hands were freezing while he retied the knot.

At night, the parachute served as a makeshift tent. A layer of pine brush spread over the snow became the base for sleeping bags, which they doubled, one inside the another. Before going to sleep, they removed their boots, slid them in between the sleeping bag layers with the hope the boots would be warm and dry by morning. One major inconvenience was the outdoor latrine. Ian still shudders at the thought of dropping a flight suit and sitting on a tree limb, butt exposed to the cold.

By day four, the crew had consumed their allotted food rations, including the onions and cabbages. When the water was gone, they melted snow. Ian recalls it took about eight cups of snow to make one cup of water. Cold and hungry, no one managed more than an hour of sleep at night. Ian, who had been used to the outdoors in Western Pennsylvania, was in excellent shape. Yet without good nourishment, he soon felt weak and starved for protein. Where to get meat? They had learned in the classroom that most four-legged animals were edible. Ian thought of a nice fat snowshoe rabbit and recalled rabbits he caught at Phillips Hall. Saliva collected in his mouth at the thought of his mother's rabbit stew. But the crew did not see any snowshoe rabbits. Most likely, earlier survival candidates had decimated them.

One event remains vivid in Ian's memory. On day five before noon, Louis spotted a porcupine on the upper branches of an 80-foot-tall pine tree, and yelled, "Food!" "We'll cook it over a low fire," someone said. They debated how best to get it down. Keith volunteered to climb the tree. A long stick in one hand, he hoisted himself up, a branch at a time, until he was almost to the top. A quick hit with his stick and the porcupine crashed down like a leaded, spiked ball. Ian was supposed to catch it but failed. The animal ended up buried in five feet of snow. Careful not to get stung by its quills, Ian dug it out, then used a heavy stick to kill it. With the three-inch blade of a Swiss Army knife, the three men took turns skinning the animal. A one-inch layer of fat surrounded its small body. It could not have weighed more than 15 pounds, the size of a small dog. Art created a makeshift tripod over a wood fire and hung a can, left-over from their food rations, and melted snow. Louis removed the porcupine's entrails, its head and paws, and cut the remaining body in small pieces. They were going to prepare porcupine stew, two batches of it because the tin can could only hold half the meat. The first batch took two hours. In anticipation Ian sniffed, tasted the broth, and discovered an unappetizing aroma of pine resin. It was getting dark when they each chewed on a small piece of meat. Ian said it reminded him of a squirrel's stringy texture with the added flavor of pine needles. He thought their effort to get a few morsels of meat was dubious, and the reward merely to have killed an animal in the wild.

For the remaining two days, the group did not scout for another animal and saved their energy to evade 'enemy' forces.

If caught, they would have been treated like prisoners and held for two days of questioning. Walking became easier as they reached the snowless eastern slopes of the Sierra Nevada. The closer they came to the base, the higher the danger of being caught. The sight of a person compelled that they drop quickly to the ground and crawl like reptiles. Once safely inside the perimeter of the base, they hurried to the mess hall and a choice of breakfast, lunch, or dinner. A shower came next, followed by another meal. Ian said he lost ten pounds that week, down to 140. But he made up for the lost calories at the dessert buffet with its freshly baked cakes, pies, and cookies.

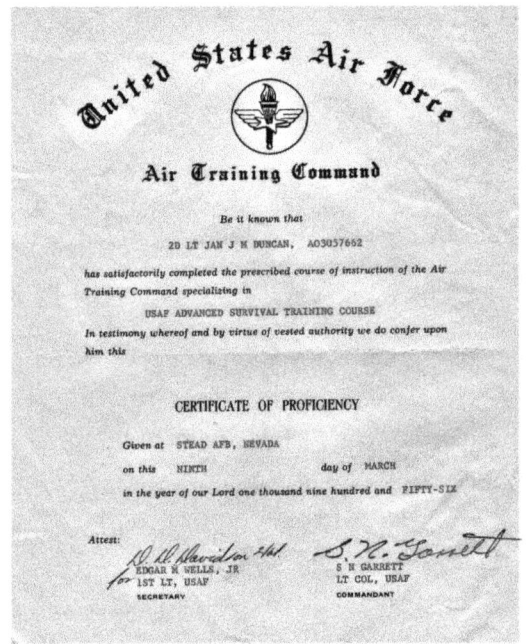

Ian's official notification of passing the U.S. Air Force Advanced Survival Training Course and being deemed "proficient."

Three years later at Avon Park, Florida, summer survival training was effortless by comparison with winter. Weather was not an issue. Ian and his crew, ten in total, cleared a 20-foot radius in the jungle to keep snakes at bay. The menu, besides a few canned rations, consisted of armadillos and lizards, both in abundance. To catch an armadillo, which could move exceedingly fast, the group split into chasers and catchers. Once caught, the armadillo retreated into itself like a turtle. Ian thought they were harder to skin than the porcupine, but the meat tasted like pork. As to a giant lizard, it was mentally not appetizing. But roasted on a spit, it tasted like chicken.

After Ian's return from Nevada to MacDill in spring 1956, he checked out on the KC-97, and practiced local refueling missions over the Gulf of Mexico. Speed control was

KC-97 refueling a B-47.

a delicate matter. The B-47 bombers approached as slowly as possible without stalling to get behind the KC-97 at 210-215 knots, the maximum speed of the tanker. Once in position, the boom operator lowered the boom, a permanent metal structure. Two elevons controlled the boom's direction into the B-47 fuel receptacle. When contact was achieved, indicator lights lit up in the bomber and tanker, and the flight engineer started the fuel transfer. Both planes then commenced a slow descent of approximately 100 feet per minute to increase the speed of the bomber, and thereby offset the weight it gained from a 15-20,000- pound fuel offload. Sometimes the tankers would refuel in formation: four tankers refueling four bombers simultaneously over water. A tricky maneuver, Ian recalled, particularly at night and during thunderstorms. On both the tanker and bomber, the words a crewmember never wanted to hear were *Break away, Break away, Break way!* Like the distress call Mayday, the words were repeated three times to ensure that they could not be mistaken. The warning call meant an imminent collision. For the tanker, this signified full power and instant ascent until 1000 feet of altitude separation. For the bomber, this meant disconnecting from the boom, and descending immediately to 1000 feet below.

In October 1956, following the Suez Canal Crisis, Ian's entire squadron was given a 70-day-assignment to Ben Guerir, an Air Base in Morocco. At the time, the United States demonstrated its regional military power with bases in Spain and North Africa.

Except for the voyage with his father to Scotland in 1939,

this was Ian's first trip abroad. The military issued a 'special passport' to be used on official business and invalid in the following countries: Albania, Bulgaria, Hungary, Egypt, Israel, Jordan, Syria, and parts of China, Korea, and Vietnam that were under communist control.

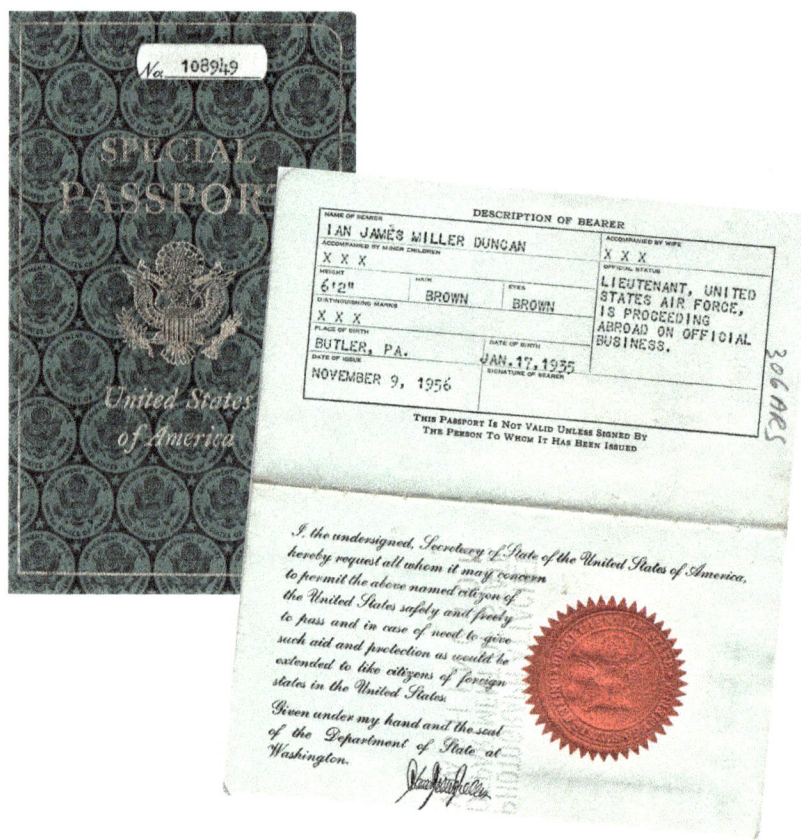

Ian's official passport.

11

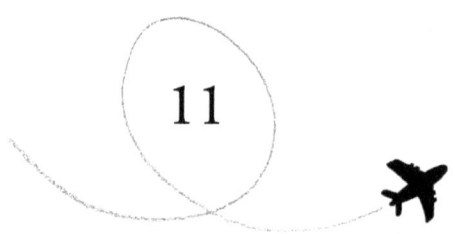

On October 17th in 1956, shortly after 7:00 p.m., twenty tankers, the entire MacDill refueling squadron, took off in ten-minute intervals. Ian was number ten. They flew in formation, 1000 feet apart, at an altitude between 10,000 and 16,000 feet, nonstop from Tampa across the mid-Atlantic to Ben Guerir Air Base, Morocco. It would take 24 hours to fly the 4,300-mile distance, the longest time Ian had piloted a plane. His commander was Bill Apgar, a Second World War veteran with a reputation of not suffering fools, but well regarded as a pilot. Ian knew that Bill had selected him as his copilot for the flight. The other crewmembers were a navigator, flight engineer, and radio operator. The boom operator also served as loadmaster to check that each item aboard was positioned correctly.

To avoid overloading the aircraft, the crews carried only the required equipment: parachutes, mosquito netting, collapsible oars, a first-aid kit, two five-man life rafts, and a 'fly-away' kit with oil filters, spark plugs, and tools in case they had to land in an area without facilities. KC-97s always needed extra oil to fill the central oil reservoir, which meant this flight had two 55-gallon metal drums on board. And because of the KC-97's normal 14-hour-fuel range, the inflight refueling tanks were filled with Avgas (Aviation gasoline). Normally, to refuel bombers, the tanks carried JP-4 (Jet Petrol-4), less expensive and less refined. Prior to this flight, the tanks had been rinsed of JP-4, and the bombers, which could use either fuel, were given Avgas. To maintain weight, balance, and the correct attitude pitch during the initial ten hours, the crew used the inflight refueling tanks to feed the engines. The KC-97s tanks could cross feed fuel. A main shut-off valve allowed access from the refueling tanks to the wing manifolds.

When I first heard about this flight, I wondered how Ian stayed alert and awake. I had been on long night flights with Pan American, though rarely more than fourteen hours. Ian said the flight surgeon had handed out pills that helped the crew stay awake. However, the pills did not guarantee 100 percent alertness, so the crew worked out a schedule to switch seats and relieve each other.

Once an hour, the radio operator contacted the lead airplane over a short-range radio. But for long distance information, such as weather for arrival in Morocco, he tapped Morse code messages via a VLF (very low frequency) radio, 20 words a minute. To send and receive such messages, the KC-97 had a 200-foot-long, weighted, trailing-wire antenna. It could be electrically reeled out of a small compartment some 50 feet forward of the tail. But at the first sight of storm clouds, the pilots had to retract the antenna because it attracted lightening.

The flight was a lengthy ordeal for the lone navigator. Ian, who knew long range navigation (Loran) and celestial navigation with a sextant, gave the navigator a reprieve that first night. The temptation to fall asleep increased when the sun rose over the eastern hemisphere, shining straight into Ian's eyes. He lit a cigarette. Anything to stay awake. Smoking was common on planes, except during refueling. Bill, the commander, who had been at the controls for the past hours, was napping. Ian kept adjusting the autopilot, which was not as reliable as on today's aircraft. Although the weather over the Atlantic was favorable that day, there was turbulence with occasional cloud formations, something the autopilot could not handle. To stay on course and maintain altitude, Ian periodically hand-flew the plane. In the morning hours, the flight engineer, who monitored the tanks, announced the inflight refueling tanks were empty and switched the manifolds to the regular tanks. By then the squadron was past Bermuda and the Eastern Antilles. An engine shut-down could be catastrophic. The only places to land were on the Azores and the Canaries. In case of a ditching, B-17 rescue planes were standing by in Bermuda and the Azores to drop life rafts.

Twelve hours into the flight, the crew had consumed the ham and cheese sandwiches. Coffee and tea in large thermos jugs were cold. There was no galley, no coffee maker, no oven. Hot cups on a counter behind the cockpit could boil water to heat pouches of ready-to-eat meals (MRE). When his commander took over the flying again, Ian was ready for breakfast and plunged a can of pre-scrambled eggs with ham into hot water. He said it was the worst meal ever.

"Worse than the porcupine?" I asked. "Close," he said.

The sun set again when they approached the North African coastline. On a recently built runway at Ben Guerir Air Base,

35 miles north of Marrakech, they landed with little fuel to spare. After a short debriefing and quick meal, Ian settled in his bed, took the sleeping pills he had received from the flight surgeon, and enjoyed a long rest.

Together with seven other officers, Ian lived in a Dallas Hut, a prefabricated 20 x 20 plywood structure with hinged panels that could be propped open for air circulation. Each hut had a bathroom and shower. Ian thanked his good fortune not to have arrived in the heat of summer. The moderate fall temperatures barely reached the mid-70s.

Ian in front of a Dallas hut at Ben Guerir, 0000.

For the following two months, time crept by. Except for one overnight trip by bus with other servicemen to Casablanca, Ian saw little of Morocco. During this one outing, the men had to be in uniform, walk in pairs, refrain from entering any establishment that served alcohol, and not engage in conversation with salespeople. Ian had not been in a souk

Ian at the nose wheel of a KC-97 in Ben Guerir.

or seen men in caftans before. He did not understand the language, felt uncomfortable, and was ready to get back to base the following day. A camel saddle stool was his only souvenir from Morocco.

There were daily briefings and lectures on weather, navigation, and recent accidents. All twenty KC-97s went through a monthly refueling circle, which meant refueling practice was limited to one tanker per day. Two tankers were always on alert status to launch in case a bomber needed fuel. Besides going to the mess hall, base exchange, and movie theater that showed a new film every second day, Ian read, played Ping-Pong, and wrote letters home.

His parents had recently left Phillips Hall and bought a ranch house in Butler. After Mr. Phillips' death earlier that year, George Duncan stayed on for a few months as chauffeur to Greta, the woman T.W. married after his first wife's death in 1945. George soon found Greta Phillips's dictatorial and disrespectful demeanor bothersome, and he sought new employment. Besides, he felt he had fulfilled his obligation to Mr. Phillips. In the summer of 1956, Magnetics, Inc., a Butler company, which made magnetic components for electronic systems, hired George to oversee their security department.

Letters were also going back and forth between Ian and his fiancé in Tampa. Two years older and savvier than Ian, B. was planning a big wedding upon his return. She lived with her parents in Tampa, in a house diagonally across the street from Ian's place. Earlier that year, Ian and his roommates had been outside when B.'s pesky little sister walked over and urged them to ask B. out. The three young men flipped a coin. Ian won. Now in Ben Guerir, 21 years old, lovesick, and horny, he bought a quarter carat diamond engagement ring at Ben Guerir's Base Exchange. A coin flip had determined his future.

Thanksgiving at Ben Guerir was a memorable event, and Ian kept the printed menu. Paper cut-out turkeys and fall

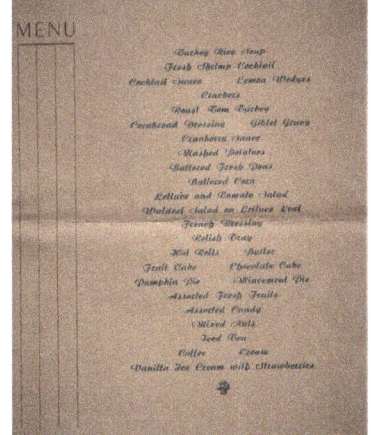

leaves decorated the mess hall's tables. There were speeches and prayers. The feast included Ian's most coveted dishes, including giblet gravy and mincemeat pie.

Just before Christmas the squadron headed home. Because of the prevailing easterly headwind, the planes could not reach Tampa nonstop. The crews would overnight at Lajes Air Base on Terciera, an island of the Azores. This coincided with Operation Safe Haven, President Eisenhower's response to the Soviet repression of the Hungarian uprising in October 1956. That December, twenty to thirty C-121 Constellations, each with Hungarian refugees en route from Munich, Germany to McGuire Airforce Base in New Jersey, landed at Lajes Air Base for refueling. Over a period of 90 days, the United States evacuated close to 30,000 Hungarian refugees, which, since the Berlin airlift, was the most significant humanitarian rescue mission.

On December 28th Shortly after his return from Ben Guerir, Ian and B. were married, a grandiose affair with bridesmaids and flowers. Ian's parents, who had not met B. earlier, were not pleased. They wished their son had waited longer before tying the knot. The young couple moved into a rental for a year. After their first child was born, they bought a new home in the same Tampa neighborhood.

In the spring of 1957, eighteen months after he received his initial commission as top graduate at Vance Air Force Base, Ian became a First Lieutenant in the United States Air Force and an aircraft commander. Bill Apgar, who had flown with Ian to

Ian at 22, aircraft commander on the KC-97.

Morocco, wrote one of the recommendations. At 22, young Ian remained lanky and thought he resembled a skeleton in a flight suit. Fellow crewmembers nicknamed him the boy-pilot. Although it could have been taken as a compliment, a still insecure Ian felt slightly offended. Each time Ian walked into Flight Operations he heard, "There's the boy-pilot to get his flight plan signed again." Not until four years later, when he had recorded 2000 flight hours, would he rank as a senior pilot. And only at this rank could he sign off on flight plans.

That same year Ian was named crew evaluator, which gave him the authority to evaluate an entire KC-97 crew. In this capacity, he had to know the flight manuals of each crewmember and their specific duties. It was an unusual position and put 22-year-old Ian into a no-win situation. Some older crewmembers did not appreciate the young lieutenant checking their flying abilities.

From October to mid-December of 1957, Ian was stationed at Thule Air Base, on the northwestern coast of Greenland. 750 miles north of the Arctic Circle, 950 miles from the North Pole, Thule is the northernmost U.S. military base. The post, built on 250 square miles, had a mess hall, a commissary, gym, library, post office, theater, chapel, hospital, BX, and Officer's club.

The first leg of the flight, MacDill to Goose Bay, Labrador, took twelve hours. After a ten-hour rest period and refueling, the flight resumed. Pilots had to carefully plan their fuel for the nine-hour-flight to Thule. Midway, there was only one alternate airport: Sondrestrom on Greenland's west coast. In case the Thule runway was closed, there were two emergency alternates on the ice fields, east and north. But Ian did not know of anyone ever using them.

Thule Air Base, Greenland.

He and his crew moved into one of the 100 barracks. Constructed with walk-in refrigerator panels, they stood on pilings to avoid shifting in the permafrost. The inside of the barracks was divided into roomettes for two to four men. They joked about living in a refrigerator box to keep warm.

Thule has only two seasons, a dark and a light one. Ian was there during the dark season when the sun's path remained largely behind the horizon, and temperatures stayed below freezing. Gale-force winds, snow and ice forced him and his crew to spend many hours inside their barracks. Phone lines were often down, and couriers sent messages to the main command building. Ian remembers Major Dave Griest, who set up a makeshift kitchen in one of the roomettes. Dave loved to cook, often served a delicious breakfast with eggs to order and pancakes for those who did not want to venture out to the mess hall. Dave also was a master bridge player and taught Ian how to play the game. No one was allowed to get off base or befriend the local population. And no females at Thule. For entertainment the military flew in a singer or a small dance group once or twice a month.

On a routine basis, each crew flew one refueling mission every two weeks. Bombers came from other bases around the North Pole. Navigation was tricky because all headings point south. Even the magnetic compass 600 miles south was unreliable. To navigate, pilots calculated directional references based on a system called GRID. I wanted to know about GRID. Ian laughed and asked if I wanted to take a three-month course!

Some B-47 bombers flew reconnaissance missions into Russia. Modified with special radio and radar equipment, the planes had so many antennas sticking from their fuselage that they resembled, in Ian's words, a porcupine. The bombers flew across the pole to survey Russian Defense. Frequently, Russian interceptors chased the planes all the way back to the runway at Thule.

Once during his assignment in Thule, Ian flew a tanker for regular maintenance to Hayes Aircraft Corporation in Birmingham, Alabama. Going south, he had a choice of laying over in Goose Bay or at Harmon Air Force Base in Stephenville, Newfoundland. Crews preferred Harmon to Goose Bay. The food was better, Ian said. But weather conditions had to be right for a nonstop flight between Thule and Harmon. After resting and refueling at Harmon, and before continuing to Birmingham, the crew loaded trash barrels with live lobsters, which cost 25 cents each. The small contingent of Air Force personnel at Hayes Aircraft had a feast.

The Distant Early Warning line (DEW line).

Ian's most memorable adventure at Thule was testing the capability of the Air Defense Command's distant early warning radar, a system of radar and communication stations extending along the DEW line (Distant Early Warning line) from Eastern Greenland to Canada's Northwest Territories. The radar stations were to detect bombers or missiles from the north.

One morning, Ian and his crew took off from Thule and climbed to 2000 feet. A second aircraft followed a mile behind, at a slightly higher altitude. The two planes headed south for two hours, and a distance of 400 nautical miles. They planned to reach their destination during the short daylight hours. As they came within 100 miles of where the radar station was supposed to be, they descended to 300 feet above ground and flew over the Arctic tundra until a big radar dome and surrounding buildings came into view. Outside, some twenty men were

123

playing volleyball. Ian could see their startled expressions as the plane buzzed the volleyball field before making an immediate left turn to the east, then headed North to Thule. Ian heard later that someone in the Air Defense Command offered the SAC commander a few drinks for letting planes penetrate the Defense's early warning radar without being detected until overhead. The incident helped to perfect the system.

In January 1958, back at MacDill, Ian passed SAC's standard evaluation training, became a check-pilot and full instructor pilot. One of Ian's most difficult decisions was to give an unsatisfactory report to his friend, Jim Gordon, another aircraft commander. The mistake occurred before take-off. Jim's crew failed to ensure that the fuel in the forward and aft tanks was of equal amount before starting the engines. To get all four running on time, this usually occurred twenty minutes before take-off. The plane's aerodynamics are affected, if 20 to 30 thousand pounds of fuel are not where they need to be and cause the center of gravity in the plane to become erratic. The check should be done before taxiing to avoid a stuck valve, which could result in the entire amount of fuel ending up in the tail and causing a huge fire. The crew was slow in their pre-flight checklist, started the engines and taxied while transferring fuel, a serious violation that made Ian call the flight unsatisfactory. Jim needed more training to get re-qualified. After that, he had a flawless career that spanned many years.

In March 1959, Ian and his crew won the tanker crew of the quarter award, a division-wide competition that scores

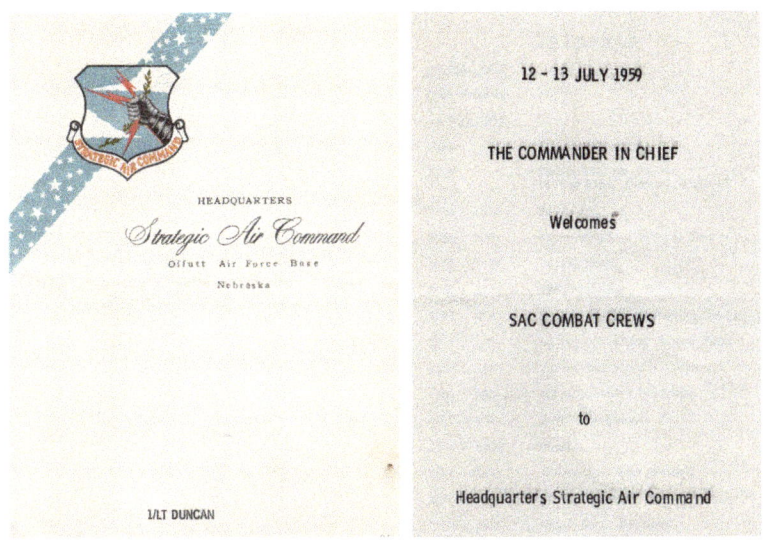

After winning the tanker crew of the quarter award, Ian and his crew were invited to the SAC headquarters at Offutt Air Force Base in Nebraska.

every aspect of flight. This resulted in an invitation to SAC headquarters at Offutt Air Force Base in Nebraska. His crew flew commercially to Omaha and spent a full day with all the high-ranking officers, including Four-star General Power. Ian thought it was a true honor to be recognized.

That same year of 1959, Ian also served a three-month on and off rotation at Harmon Air Force Base, Newfoundland. SAC had moved a part of its bomber and aerial refueling aircraft to 24-hour alert status, ready to take off from designated sites within fifteen minutes. Bombers flying to Europe needed refueling over the North Atlantic. Until he retired from the active Air Force in April 1960, Ian spent half of his time, summer and winter, at Harmon, prepared to take off on a 15-minute notification. The planes were 'hot', cocked like guns ready to fire. Within five minutes of getting in the cockpit, all four engines had to be running. The first plane taxiing became the lead, the second two minutes later. Conditions in winter were often hazardous, with huge amounts of ice and snow. During extremely cold temperatures, switches in the cockpit helped pilots dilute the oil tanks with fuel. Ian said that without thinning the oil, a pilot could wear out starters. The added fuel burned off as the oil cycled through the engines. Ian said the flying conditions that winter of 1959/1960 had been the worst in his career.

I mentioned earlier in this chapter that the KC-97s central oil tank needed replenishing during long flights. Without lubrication and careful survey of the oil supply, the engines would eventually fail. Ian recalled an accident in March 1960. A KC-97 crew from Newfoundland to MacDill ran low on oil. Six hours into the flight, the oil in the two 55-gallon drums was gone. Why the commander did not request a re-routing to Charleston, or another East Coast Air Force base, remains a mystery. By the time the flight was an hour from MacDill, low-oil-pressure warning lights forced the crew to execute a controlled ditching off Florida's eastern coast. The KC-97, thanks to its tight fuselage, had a high floating capability. All crewmembers survived except for the radio operator, a man Ian knew and respected. While the crew awaited rescue, the radio operator had stepped out on the wing to check propeller and engine damage. A wave caused him to slip. He hit his head on a propeller, fractured his skull, and drowned. A sad moment in KC-97's history. The Coast Guard eventually sank the plane because it was a hazard to navigation.

As a KC-97 commander, Ian did not encounter any such incidents. He enjoyed his time at Harmon Air Base and carried home lobsters after each rotation. Still, an airline career remained foremost in his mind. During a visit with his parents in Butler, he spoke with Mr. Scholter and met up with former students, Ray White and Roger Whitesell. By then they were copilots, flying Viscounts for Capital Airlines. They raved about their earnings, claimed more money than Ian's military pay, and urged Ian to apply. Although Ian was a regular officer in the Air Force and in time would move up in rank, he feared that he would not be just a pilot but have to assume administrative desk jobs. As an airline pilot, he would be doing what he loved most: flying. Little did he know then that an airline career would eventually draw him into a desk. Ian's final flight in the Air Force was April 21st, 1960. He would continue for another sixteen years in the Air National Guard.

12

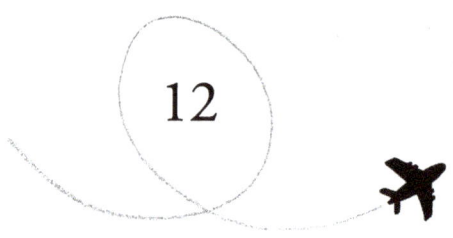

In February 1960, Ian applied to several airlines. Few were hiring new pilots. When they did, it was during peak travel from April to September. Then, as soon as travel lessened, the companies sent furlough notices. Capital Airlines, a mainstream East Coast air carrier with a crew base in Pittsburgh, hired Ian in March and trained him at Washington National airport as a DC-3 co-pilot. He commuted from Tampa to Pittsburgh and, when in town, stayed with his parents in Butler.

The flying was sparse. Ian's pilot logbook from May 1960, shows only six flights between Pittsburgh, Erie, and Charleston, West Virginia. At the time, Capital's financial problems were making the news. The company had bought a fleet of Vickers

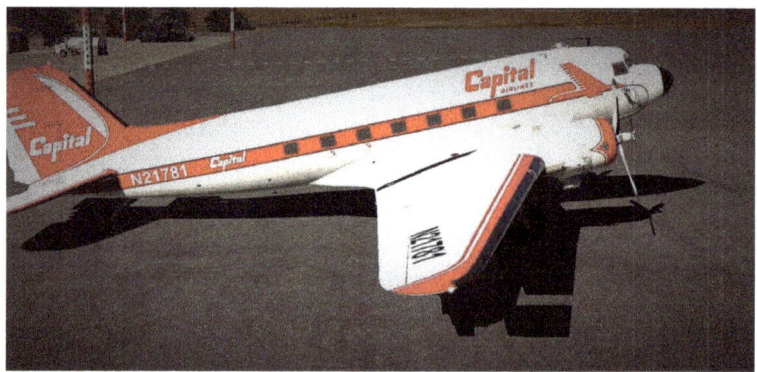

Capital DC-3.

Viscounts, a British turboprop plane, an expensive aircraft to fly and maintain. The Viscounts operated at a loss unless more than half of its seats were occupied. Plus, the planes had a less than stellar history. There had been crashes related to structure, loose bolts, landing gear failures, wings and tails falling off. Between 1958 and 1960, Capital's Viscounts had four fatal crashes. Today, Ian wonders how the Viscount ever received certification.

In May 1960, Vickers foreclosed on Capital's entire fleet of Viscounts. Bankruptcy seemed unavoidable. The lack of flying worried Ian, particularly at the onset of Capital's peak season. The new captains were demoted to co-pilots. Ian, unsure what to do, consulted his old Air Force friend, Keith, who was flying DC-3s for Southern Airways in Atlanta. Keith encouraged Ian to apply at Southern, said the airline would be eager to hire him because of his DC-3 qualification. Before the end of May, barely two months after starting with Capital, Ian and some sixty newly hired pilots received furlough notices.

Southern hired Ian immediately. He moved to Atlanta, started a week-long ground school, a requirement with all airlines regardless of a pilot's experience. Before Ian's week was over, Southern Airways pilots voted to strike over wages. Disappointed and feeling uneasy, Ian opted to stay in Atlanta, hopeful the strike would end soon. He could not have predicted a dispute that would drag on for two years. Meanwhile, the Air Line Pilot Association (ALPA) had secured an agreement with Southern Airline's management for all recently hired pilots to keep their seniority, but only if they did not fly as strike breakers. This is how

Ian ended up walking the picket line. As a new-hire, he had not yet received his uniform. The one he borrowed from a friend fit badly. The pants barely reached his ankles.

It was the longest and costliest strike in ALPA's history. Southern Airways refused to negotiate and meet with the union's representatives. The company hired new pilots, mostly former Second World War veterans, who were eager to work. Within two months, Southern was fully operational again. To walk the picket line, ALPA gave each pilot a monthly 300-dollar strike payment. To cover Southern pilots' benefits,

Ian on the picket line for striking Southern Airways.

ALPA charged all members flying for other airlines, 75 to 100 dollars per paycheck. Strangely, in Ian's case, he made more money with strike pay than as a new-hire for Southern. Yet compared to his former monthly 700-dollar Air Force income, the paycheck was meager, particularly after the arrival of his second son, James Ian, in May 1960.

I asked Ian if he had regrets about leaving the Air Force that year. Ian said he hadn't. I asked how he'd kept a positive attitude. With a pensive expression, Ian said he never lost hope. He felt that sooner or later he would become a successful airline pilot. Seniority was his pot of gold. Senior pilots would eventually retire, and at 25, he was young enough to wait.

Regardless of financial instability, Ian rented a small duplex, moved his family from Tampa to Atlanta, and joined the 102nd Air Transport Squadron of the Georgia National Guard. With his background as a KC-97 tanker pilot, the Guard immediately accepted Ian as a commander on the C-97, a cargo version of the KC-97. In months to come he transported heavy equipment, such as small trucks, propellers, and barrels of oil to Europe, Central America, Hawaii, and Alaska. Ian took his responsibilities as a commander seriously. He tended to his crew first and made certain they had food and quarters upon arrival. On his first return flight from Panama, Ian and his crew, all ten of them, paid one dollar each for a stalk of bananas and hung them from the C-97's ceiling. I said, "Lobsters from Newfoundland, bananas from Panama? What else?" Ian answered with, "Bags of Hawaiian macadamia nuts and Mateus Rosé from Portugal."

A noteworthy event happened on a flight from Florida to Kentucky. Ian was transporting personnel but planned to be home in Atlanta that evening. Somewhere over the Appalachians the aircraft headed into dark clouds and thunderstorms. Ian suddenly heard a bang, causing his heart to skip a beat. But nothing indicated that something was wrong. Then the loadmaster entered the cockpit and told Ian that he had seen what resembled an orange ball of fire going down the center aisle, then exiting the tail. People in the cabin were shaking. But no one was hurt, and there did not seem to be any damage. The flight continued to Lexington. Upon landing, the crew discovered that a static discharge had burnt a hole in the upper rudder. Fabric was flapping, the rudder beyond repair. A new one took three days to arrive, and none of the crew had an overnight bag. Sometime later, Ian shared this incident with pilots, who had experienced a similar problem. It was agreed that all of them had been flying around 11,000 feet altitude and close to an outside air temperature of zero degrees Celsius. At the time, however, no scientific studies existed to explain the problem.

That winter of 1961, Ian had an opportunity to visit relatives in Scotland. He was scheduled to fly a C-97 from Atlanta to Rhein-Main Air Base in Germany. A 30-hour layover at Prestwick Airport near Glasgow meant there was enough time to see his aunt and uncles. Ian's parents were more than excited. George placed a call to his brother William in Edinburgh. Ian loved imitating his father's Scottish brogue: "Willie, mah laddie is comin' tae see ye. Ian's a captain in th' Air Force, flies a huge airplane." This was big news for Willie who immediately phoned his brother Jimmy and sister Nan. Friends and neighbors were alerted. Ian laughed and imitated what would have been said. "Come 'n' catch up wi' oor nephew, th' pilot, wha comes flying fae America."

Ian landed in Prestwick on a cold February morning, changed quickly from his flight suit to his blue Air Force uniform. Then he rode to the train station and called Uncle Willie from a pay phone to give an approximate time of his arrival. On the train, people took notice of young Ian in his uniform. Where was he going? Was he stationed in Scotland? Happy to make conversation, Ian told a brief version of his family's history. Four hours later, after switching trains in Glasgow, he arrived in Edinburgh, bought a large box of candy, and took a taxi to Uncle Willie's apartment. Beneath an overcast sky, Edinburgh looked unfriendly and cold. As the taxi drove to the outskirts of town, Ian watched for some landmark, anything that would recall his visit as a four-year-old with his father in 1939. Nothing looked familiar.

The taxi stopped in front of a two-story building. No sooner had Ian stepped from the car, than his uncles, dressed in their Sunday best, came out to greet him. Willie and Jimmy must have been by the window, watching for his arrival. In the living room, Aunt Nan was arranging a tea set on a rectangular table, covered with an embroidered linen cloth. Looking up at Ian, she said, "Ye hae gotten lanky sin ah lest saw ye." As the foursome sat around the table, she poured tea into cups, opened a tin of MacFarlane Lang biscuits, and passed the box of candy. Ian glanced around the room, which a small fireplace kept comfortably warm. The décor was working class, yet cozy. Velvety chairs had arm and head rests. A few old photos hung on papered walls. Uncle Willie, unmarried and four years younger than Ian's father, wanted to know every detail about the big plane Ian flew. Jimmy, recently widowed, inquired about life in America, about Ian's parents and children. Aunt Nan, an old spinster, was quick to say that she never forgave her brother George for leaving his clan. Soon the doorbell chimed, bringing in a parade of friendly neighbors to meet th' famous pilot fae America. Ian did not like being placed on a pedestal. But that day he happily accepted the adoration. He talked about his long flight, the navigation, and where he was off to next. As the day waned and darkness set in, the visitors left. Jimmy and Nan took a bus back to their homes. Uncle Willie and Ian visited a bit longer, had a snack of cold cuts, cheese, and a glass of port. Before going to bed, Willie took two pieces of coal from the fireplace, put them into an asbestos bag and placed it under Ian's bedsheets. By morning, without central heat, the room was as frigid as an ice cellar. Not since winter survival training had Ian felt this cold. He dressed quickly, bade his uncle farewell, and hurried to the station. His flight left that afternoon for Germany, then on to Naples, Madrid, and the Azores. A week later Ian was back home and phoned his parents, said his uncles and aunt looked well, spoke about the warm welcome he had received. But he also mentioned the cold, the austere living conditions, the lack of private transportation. Having seen this, he now understood why his father left the old country and came to the United States. By contrast, Ian's parents, then in their early sixties, had prospered. They owned a ranch house with central heat, and Ian's father drove his own car, a 1959 Ford sedan.

George and Isabella received letters from Scotland with rave reviews aboot thair laddie. Uncle Willie and Aunt Nan died before Ian could see them again. Nearly three decades passed before Ian and I saw Uncle Jimmy one last time in Edinburgh.

Back in Atlanta the strike continued. ALPA and Southern had not reached an agreement, and Ian's airline career looked grim. From time to time, when short of money, Ian resorted to selling stocks that remained in Mr. Phillip's trust fund. Once again, he quietly thanked his benefactor. Then a Western Union telegram arrived:

```
EA WUA036 PD
          WUX WASHINGTON DC VIA BUTLER PENN APR 11
I J DUNCAN
9670 MONTVIEW BLVD*10C AURORA COLO
RECALL FROM FURLOUGH. REPORT TO PILOT RECORDS OFFICE
WASHINGTON NO LATER THAN APRIL 24, 1961. ACKNOWLEDGE BY
RETURN WIRE OR TELEPHONE. PRESENT THIS TELEGRAM TO DOM
FOR TRANSPORTATION.
     IF UAL FLIGHT ENGINEER TRAINING COMPLETE REPORT SOON
AS POSSIBLE. IF PRESENTLY IN UAL FLIGHT ENGINEER
SCHOOL YOU ARE TO COMPLETE SCHOOL BEFORE REPORTING.
YOU WILL BE ON CAP PAYROLL AND EXPENSES EFFECTIVE APRIL
24, 1961.
     IF SCHEDULED TO ENTER UAL FLIGHT ENGINEER SCHOOL
YOU WILL BE ON CAP PAYROLL EFFECTIVE THE DATE OF THIS
RECALL.
     CAPITAL AIRLINES H MJ REID.
600PM..
```

> RECALL FROM FURLOUGH. REPORT TO PILOT RECORD OFFICE WASHINGTON NO LATER THAN APRIL 24, 1961. ACKNOWLEDGE BY RETURN WIRE OR TELEPHONE. PRESENT THIS TELEGRAM TO DOM* FOR TRANSPORTATION.
>
> IF UAL FLIGHT ENGINEER TRAINING COMPLETE REPORT SOON AS POSSIBLE.
>
> IF PRESENTLY IN UAL FLIGHT ENGINEER SCHOOL YOU ARE TO COMPLETE SCHOOL BEFORE REPORTING. YOU WILL BE ON CAPITAL PAYROLL AND EXPENSES EFFECTIVE APRIL 24, 1961
>
> IF SCHEDULED TO ENTER FLIGHT ENGINEER SCHOOL, YOU WILL BE ON CAPITAL PAYROLL THE DATE OF THIS RECALL.
>
> CAPITAL AIRLINES   H MJ REID.

*District Operation Manager

I could not make sense of this. Ian was going to work as a flight engineer for Capital Airlines, which had merged with United Airlines, while still on strike with Southern?

Ian explained what had happened: In July 1960, after Ian's furlough from Capital, the Civil Aeronautics Board approved the merger of Capital Airlines with United, which wanted Capital's routes to Florida. The merger, then the largest in history, was completed on June 1st, 1961. United, ready to replace its fleet of DC-3s and Viscounts with DC-7s and DC-6s, needed pilots and flight engineers to fly the newly acquired planes. Without telling Southern of his intention, Ian accepted the recall. No longer on the picket line, he had to forego his monthly ALPA strike pay. With a slight emotional quiver, Ian recalls how his friends at Southern organized a collection, which gave him 250 dollars to live on until his first paycheck from Capital. Ian departed for Denver, United's training facility,

In Denver, Ian reconnected with former Capital pilots. They lived in a boarding house, run by a gracious, grandmotherly woman, who charged each trainee 60 dollars a week for room and board. A self-proclaimed food connoisseur in his later years, Ian recalls the meals as tasty and wholesome. Flight engineer training on the DC-6/7 took six weeks. Unlike requalifying as a co-pilot, the course was longer, with more emphasis on electrical and hydraulic systems, fuel, heating, and air-conditioning. With almost identical cockpit layouts, the DC-6 and DC-7s resembled siblings. Yet the DC-7 had bigger engines, flew faster, had a higher take-off gross weight, and carried more passengers and cargo.

With training completed, Ian was re-assigned to Pittsburgh and began flying the DC-6 as a reserve flight engineer. He moved his family from Atlanta to a rental house in Coraopolis, not far from the Pittsburgh airport. Although Ian was happy to be back with an airline, he earned little money. His first paystub dated May 5th, 1961, shows net earnings of $ 125.86 (around $ 1,100 in today's market). Until the company's merger on June 1st, Ian remained a Capital employee.

Ian's Capital Airlines pay stub.

From June 1961 to October of the following year, Ian worked as a flight engineer for United. Although based in Pittsburgh, he replaced more senior flight engineers on vacation, and often spent a month temporarily in Chicago, Detroit, or New York.

Then in September 1962, the Southern Airways dispute was settled. Southern management had used public funds and

Ian's United Airlines identification card.

subsidies to absorb the cost of its labor dispute for recruiting, training, and replacing employees engaged in a lawful strike. The Southern Airline founder and president finally capitulated when an investor, in order to end the strike, threatened to sell a controlling stake to ALPA. For decades to come, the union used this victory as an example on how smaller airlines could protect their pilots' wages.

When Ian heard the news, he faced a dilemma. Go back to flying DC-3s for Southern, or remain a flight engineer on the DC-7 with United? Which would be the safer deal? He liked working for United, the larger air carrier, but he feared another furlough. Word had gotten around that United was going to phase out DC-7s and replace them with DC-8s, the first four-engine jet, which could fly nonstop from coast to coast with twice the cargo and passengers. Yet Ian was also uncertain about Southern. How would the small Atlanta-based airline face competition in the future? For a month, Ian vacillated. And to learn more about United's plans, he made an appointment with his chief pilot in Pittsburgh. Ian recalls a 15-minute conversation, in which his chief pilot confirmed what Ian feared, that his DC-7 flight engineer position might soon be eliminated. Yet Ian was unprepared to cut his ties to United and asked for an unpaid leave of absence. After his request was denied, Ian resigned. He moved his family back to Atlanta and requalified as a co-pilot on Southern DC-3s and Martin-404s.

On January 31st, 1963, Ian flew his first trip as a Southern Airways co-pilot from Atlanta to Columbus, Mississippi. The plane landed during a massive snowstorm after three circling approaches. Ian said he enjoyed the short routes, 100 to 250 miles between cities. In good weather, he flew visual without instruments, the way he had flown in his youth. It was still legal for airlines to fly under VFR (visual flight rules). In later years, to avoid airborne collisions, Federal Aviation Regulations implemented instrument flying. By November that year, he was senior enough to exclusively fly the Martin-404 on routes from Atlanta to Jacksonville, Florida, or Huntsville, Alabama. This meant more pay. For the first time in his airline career, Ian felt secure in his job. He liked Southern Airways, a small airline where pilots knew one another. Then, on January 21, 1964, an unfortunate incident occurred.

That afternoon, Ian and Captain Bill C. flew from Atlanta to Huntsville. Their 7:00 p.m. arrival coincided with another flight from New Orleans, piloted by Captain Al G., a friend of Bill's. Both in their forties, Bill and Al had known each other a long time. On the way to the hotel, Bill stopped and bought a quart of bourbon. He invited his friend Al, the co-pilots, and two female flight attendants to his room for a drink. Everyone went. But Al's co-pilot, a non-drinker, stayed for twenty minutes and left. The flight attendants went to their room when the two captains, slightly buzzed, began telling war stories. Ian, after one drink, was the next to leave. The following morning, in the hotel's lobby, both captains reeked of alcohol. A concerned clerk at the front desk took Ian aside and said, "I hope you're flying the plane back to Atlanta." Before getting in the plane, Bill asked Ian if he could handle the flight by himself, then fell asleep in his cockpit seat. Ian flew the plane safely to Atlanta, then continued that same day with a different captain to Scranton, Pennsylvania. That night, Ian assumed the incident was forgotten.

Here I must mention something to the reader. In those years, airlines did not have observers to follow a crew and check for alcohol. Nowadays, a co-pilot would be required to cancel the flight. But then crewmembers covered for each other. Four years later, when flying for Pan American, I witnessed the same occurrence on rare occasions. Just as Ian had done then, crewmembers upheld an unwritten rule of loyalty.

A few days after the January incident, Ian's chief pilot called and asked for a meeting. Ian wanted to know why. The chief pilot mentioned a letter of complaint about a drunk captain, who had done damage to a room in Huntsville. The motel's owner wrote that a maid had found an empty bourbon bottle, an ice bucket on the bed, a broken lamp, and a baggage holder without legs. Not sure what this meant for him, Ian called co-pilot friends, related what he knew of two captains getting drunk on a lay-over in Huntsville. Apparently the two had held an ice-throwing contest, broken some furniture, and fought with each other until the quart of bourbon was empty. Although Ian had been legal to fly the following morning, with eight hours between 'bottle and throttle', as the saying goes, he felt guilty by association. Before he was to meet with the chief pilot and the company's lawyers, Ian spoke with ALPA representatives. They debated whether to send their lawyers to the meeting to instruct Ian about what to say. In the end, ALPA decided that Ian was innocent, should go alone, and advised him to tell the truth.

The meeting took place in mid-February. Ian related how, that evening of January 21st, he spent a short time with both captains, had one drink, went to his room, and watched a specific TV show. When asked about the demeanor of both captains the following morning, Ian said they looked as if they had not slept. Again, Ian avoided badmouthing his fellow crewmembers. He did not think that it was up to him to declare them drunkards. As a result, pending further investigation, Ian and both captains were dismissed from the airline. Ian felt as if a missile hit him.

In the coming weeks and months, and depending on the day, Ian's feelings went from frustration to hopefulness, then back to desperation. He slept poorly, smoked excessively. Often, he regretted not having cancelled the flight out of Huntsville. Without income and to make ends meet, he flew as often as possible in the Georgia Air National Guard. He also accepted a part-time job, flying a Piper Aztec for Atlanta Tile and Marble. The company specialized in non-static tile and marble floors, used exclusively in hospitals to avoid an electrical charge on shoes and clothing. In all, the investigation lasted four months. The stewardess on Ian's flight attested that Ian had consumed only one drink. The arbitrator took five weeks to enter an opinion, which resulted in both captains losing their jobs. But Ian was absolved. Southern management gave him a date to become re-current on the DC-3 and Martin 404. But by then, Ian already had something better in mind.

In the spring of 1964, while the investigation took place, Ian flew on an Air National Guard flight with Bill Davis, an Eastern Airlines captain. Bill said rumors were circulating around Eastern cockpits that Pan American World Airways, for the first time since 1955, was hiring pilots. "If I were younger," Bill said," I would apply at once." He added that Pan American would be interested in Ian's experience as a pilot and greatly value his flight engineer/navigator's licenses. Finally, the chance Ian had waited for! To fly for a major international carrier. He called Pan American, asked for an application, sent it back, waited to be called for an interview. When, in late May he had not heard, Ian called Pan American's personnel office and spoke to Judy Reid, the assistant personnel director at JFK.

She told Ian that his name had not yet been selected for an interview, that Pan American could only test a limited number of candidates on a given day. If, however, he wanted to take the chance as a walk-in, he could just show up. Applicants with an appointment often canceled at the last minute. And because testing examiners were paid regardless, Ian could fill an open slot. "Come to Pan American's Hangar-14 at JFK Airport and see me."

On Sunday, May 31st, Ian flew to New York. He hoped to get a hotel room near the airport, so he could arrive at the personnel office early on Monday morning. But rooms were hard to find. The 1964 New York World Fair was in full swing. A cab driver said he knew of a hotel with vacancies in Manhattan. Only after Ian had slipped the front desk clerk a 10-dollar bill, said he was an airline employee and would leave at dawn, was he given a room. Arriving at Hangar-14 the following morning, Ian met with Judy Reid, a pleasant young woman in her twenties. She had good news. Three applicants had cancelled. Ian would undergo an interview and medical exam that same day. The second day, he would complete tests for English and Math knowledge, retention of information, and his skills with people. Ian refers to the exam as an early Human Factors assessment, with Pan American in a position to select the best people.

Two weeks later, on June 15th, Ian received a telegram to report to the Chief Flight Engineer at Hangar-14 and start training on July 6. Pan American had hired him as a student flight engineer on the Boeing 707, his first jet aircraft.

For the past four years, this was the break Ian hoped might happen. And being in the first group of new hires gave him a considerable jump in seniority. Ian did not pilot another flight for Southern Airways. He packed all belongings in a trailer, moved his family to a rental house in New Jersey, and shared an apartment near JFK airport with three new trainees.

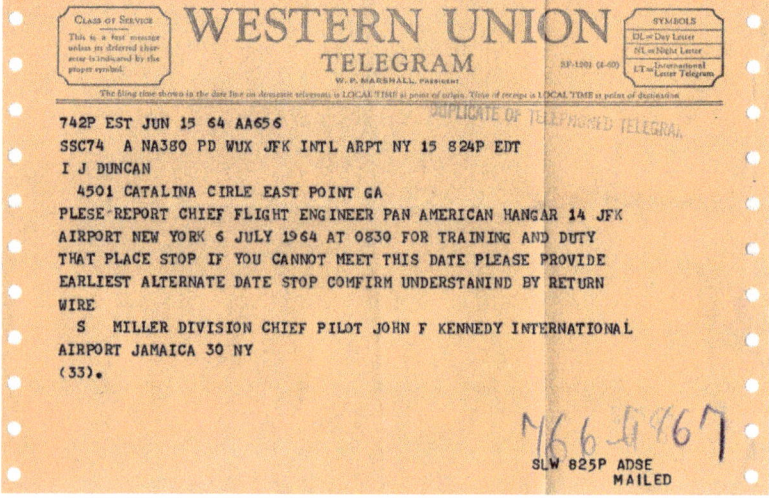

Above: *Pan American's telegram to Ian.* Below: *Copy of Ian's telegram response to Pan American.*

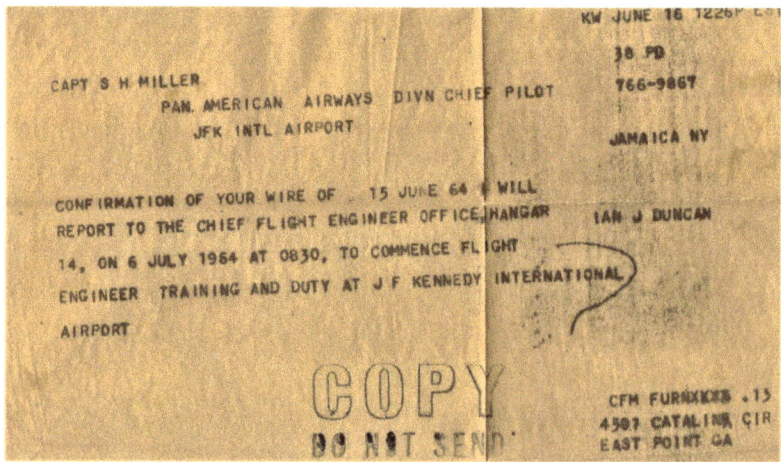

Four years later, the reader may be interested to know, I walked into the same Pan American Hangar-14. At the time I lived in Bermuda, where the director of Pan American's sales office in Hamilton, Bermuda's capital, suggested I interview to become a stewardess. At the time this was a highly coveted job for young women who spoke languages and had a college degree. The director gave me a pass to fly to JFK, and he alerted the personnel office at Hangar-14. But Ian and I would not meet until 1970. In the interim, Ian sought sexual freedom beyond marriage and engaged in multiple amorous adventures.

13

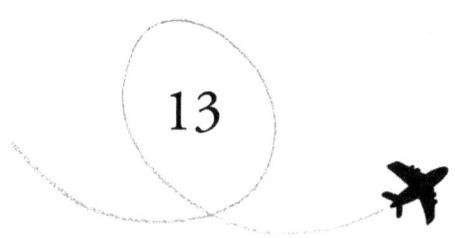

In the summer of 1960, a Delta Airlines stewardess approached Ian inside the Atlanta terminal building, where he was picketing for striking Southern Airways pilots. With a flirtatious smile, she said she had not seen Ian before. Was he new on the picket line? Ian told her that pilots walked in shifts, sometimes on the sidewalk outside Southern Airways headquarters, and other times inside the terminal, which also served Delta and Eastern Airlines. She told Ian she had come off a flight, thought he needed nourishment, and handed him an airsick bag with finger sandwiches. "Leftover from first class," she said, then left without telling him her name. As Ian watched her stride away, he thought nice body, then bit into a sandwich. Yet it puzzled him why the young woman had approached him and not the other three men on the picket line. Had she felt sorry for him? A young, unemployed pilot who resembled bozo the tramp in baggy, hand-me-down uniform trousers that barely reached his ankles. He assumed he would not see her again and put the Delta stewardess out of his mind.

Four days later, Ian was picketing on the sidewalk that ran from Southern headquarters to their maintenance hangars. It was not unusual for cars to stop. People were curious and wanted to know about the strike, which had not made the headlines in Atlanta newspapers. But that day Ian saw a familiar face. The same young woman pulled her car close to the sidewalk, rolled the window down, and said, "I see you're still at it." With a facetious grin, Ian said he had to endure Atlanta's steamy hot summer so he could receive a union strike paycheck. He heard her say that next time, she would bring more sandwiches and a drink. Two days later she returned and asked Ian how soon he would be off duty. "Half an hour," he said. She offered to take him to her place for a sandwich and iced tea. Naïve Ian accepted. I had to ask if he really believed the young woman had invited him for a sandwich? He claimed naiveté again.

Her name was Julie, an attractive, unattached 19-year-old from Louisiana, who had been with Delta for six months. Although she had seen Ian's wedding band, Julie proposed they meet again. Several dates later, Julie invited Ian to a well-prepared candlelight dinner. Ian liked the attention and fell for the romance, which was missing in his marriage.

In 1960, when 25-year-old Ian joined the airlines, he had not shed the boy-pilot image of his Air Force years. Cockpits, hangars, flight schools, clubs, and the USAF community were a male realm. And except for Joanne, his high school sweetheart, and the fling with Tammy, Ian seldom sought the companionship of females. Then at 21, he married. In his mind this was the only moral way for a permanent sexual relationship. Yet soon his marriage was in trouble. Except for their sons, he and his wife had few common interests. By the time Ian started flying for the airlines, he realized his irrevocable mistake, though religious upbringing taught him that divorce was a sin. It took ten more years for Ian to overcome his guilty conscience and leave the marriage.

Ian's belated coming of age coincided with a social movement in the early sixties that challenged codes of sexual behavior. Women objected to being treated as 'the second sex' and took charge of their sexuality. No need, in other words, for Ian to pursue the young air hostess. She approached him with clear intentions. And Ian, ready to make up for lost time in his youth, set out to discover what he could learn about the opposite sex. Julie was only the beginning.

When Ian had been in his teens, sex was not discussed. His parents never mentioned the subject, and the church considered premarital sex immoral. Sexual education in school took the form of scare tactics about harmful and adverse consequences. When Ian was an 18-year-old instructor at Scholter Aviation, he worked with a mechanic named Bob. In his thirties, Bob was married to a beautiful woman. At the time Ian wondered what attracted her to the buck-toothed, already gray-haired Bob, other than his sense of humor and quick wit. On occasion, Bob and Ian ate lunch together in the anteroom of the repair shop. Their conversation sometimes turned to sex, and Bob became Ian's mentor on this formerly taboo subject. This was in the early 1950s, when the Kinsey Report on male and female sexual behavior made the news. On August 24th, 1953, Dr. Kinsey appeared on Time's cover. An accompanying feature article concluded that Kinsey had done for sex what Columbus did for geography. That same year, Bob enlightened curious Ian on the erotic pleasures of love making.

By his late 20s, Ian recognized his effect on women. Young females took a liking to the tall pilot with auburn hair and dark brown eyes, which given the right light, gave a glint of gold. When looking at people, Ian had a way of tilting his head downward and raising his eyes to generate a boyish, mischievous smile. Nothing affectatious about it. He showed confidence without appearing superior. Women fell for his charm. And without saying a word, he had their attention.

Soon the innocent looking boy-pilot was no longer naïve. He knew what women wanted from him and basked in the sexual freedom. From 1960 to 1970, Ian engaged in mating games that grew in proportion to the size of the cockpit, from the DC-3 to the Boeing-707! One could hardly avoid contact in the cockpit of a DC-3. A stewardess might brush her arm against Ian's head while handing him a beverage. A close encounter in the galley could lead to more flirtation. Nowadays, this behavior is labeled sexual harassment. In the 1960s, males and females generally regarded coquetry as friendliness.

For United Airlines' DC-6 crews, the place to party was Buffalo, New York. While a flight engineer, Ian's schedule took him frequently from Chicago to Buffalo, with a long layover. He recalls that stewardesses made special arrangements to be on his flights. A simple friendly conversation often led to a sexual encounter in someone's room. The number of onboard stewardesses grew with the airplane's size. This had the potential to result in an awkward situation. What was Ian to do if two paramours showed up on the same flight? His answer was to lock the cockpit and ignore any knocks on his hotel room door.

Ian's love affairs peaked during his initial years with Pan American. The extensive route structure with long lay-overs in exotic places created fertile ground for romantic encounters. Whether on African beaches, Caribbean Islands, the Hilton in Tehran, the Intercontinental hotels in Frankfurt and Bangkok, crewmembers found ways to party. Affairs flourished until a trip ended. Then it was time to return to the reality of home. A unique playground was Chicago, a small base for only stewardesses. Ian, by then a first officer for Pan Am, flew double Atlantic crossings from New York to London or Frankfurt, then on to Chicago and back. On his Chicago approach charts he kept names and phone numbers of stewardesses. Whoever was the first to answer his call had the date. But women talk, and soon Ian had a reputation as a Don Juan. Before getting into more trouble, he sought different routes.

Most of Pan American's pilots were middle-aged in 1964 when 29-year-old Ian began flying for the airline. His class of youthful new hires appealed to Pan American's stewardesses, who were in their early twenties and had to be single. Many were foreign born, smart, well-educated, and good conversationalists. Ian welcomed not only their openness toward sex, but also their curiosity about his flying career, the books he read, his choices in art and music. These were not subjects that interested his wife.

In 1970, on a flight from Rome to Beirut, Ian tried to

charm me with a silly request for coffee. I was not amused and remained distant. He later admitted that my unresponsiveness had aroused his curiosity. I was different and did not fawn over Ian (Jim) Duncan. He realized that to know me better, he would have to modify his approach. Fortunately, he did.

14

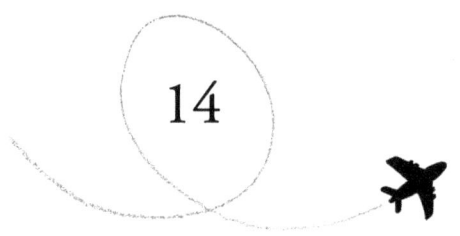

From September 1964 until August 1965, Ian was a pilot/flight engineer for Pan American. Prior to 1961, the airline only employed professional flight engineers, who were not pilots. The new position was established following a dispute between the Flight Engineer International Association (FEIA) and the Air Line Pilot Association (ALPA). FEIA argued that an airline should not qualify pilots as engineers unless they had an FAA issued airframe and powerplant (A&P) certificate. ALPA disputed the claim and recommended that airlines train pilots as flight engineers without an A&P license. A pilot/flight engineer, according to ALPA, was more valuable because he could relieve the captain or co-pilot in an emergency. Each union claimed its position as not self-serving. At the time, however, the consensus was that FEIA hoped to preserve the membership of its flight engineers. In the end, Nathan Feinsinger, the chairman of President Kennedy's Commission, determined that neither peace nor safety would be assured when there were two unions in the cockpit. The Commission ordered the airlines to pay the costs for professional flight engineers to receive pilot training. An expensive undertaking. Professional flight engineers, many of whom were in their fifties, had two choices: to retire early, or receive a commercial and instrument rating. Only a small number ever became airline pilots, and Ian thinks not many harbored the ambition.

On the B-707, Ian's workstation was behind the co-pilot's seat. As a flight engineer, he faced a large panel of switches, knobs, and push buttons. His table was wide enough to hold the in-flight fuel monitoring log and a meal tray. During take-off and landing, Ian swiveled his seat to the central position behind both pilots and monitored engine power, exhaust gas temperature, and maximum engine RPM.

Pan American's B-707 cockpit.

During each hour inflight, Ian noted in his engineer's flight log, the generator outputs, hydraulic pressure, and fuel. And if necessary, he applied fuel heat. Another duty was to maintain a comfortable cabin temperature, which depended on the passenger load. A partially empty cabin required more heat output. Ian also kept cabin pressure at a suitable level. With a grin, he told me that a rise above 8.6 PSI in pressure could blow out windows and doors. The thought made me shudder and I asked if he was kidding. Ian reassured me that all airplanes have a preset valve that automatically releases over-pressurized air to prevent a disaster.

Another element of Ian's duties as flight engineer was to monitor the flight from a pilot's point of view. He provided an extra pair of eyes for the purpose of avoiding mistakes. In case the pilot, who was not flying the take-off or approach, omitted correct speed and altitude call-outs, Ian served as back-up. And before a descent, Ian drew a profile from the captain's or co-pilot's Jeppesen approach plate (pilot navigation chart) and filled the important points of altitude and heading to show how the approach and landing should be executed. Each airport was different. Runways had various lengths and widths. Although most airports of that era were equipped with ILS (instrument landing systems) and provided directional and flight path control, several offered no vertical guidance and required non-precision approaches. Guatemala City, Lagos in Nigeria, and Rangoon (now Yangon, Myanmar) were among those. Other airports had even more restrictions. A captain on his first approach into Rio de Janeiro, San Jose (Costa Rica), and Hong Kong had to be monitored by an FAA approved check airman.

There was always concern about an engine failure after take-off, which required dumping fuel to reduce the plane's maximum landing weight (as determined by Boeing and the runway's length). Because of long over-sea routes, most Pan American flights carried a full load of fuel. But even for shorter distances, some flights 'tankered' fuel to avoid a higher price at the next stop.

An incident occurred on September 5th, 1964, shortly after taking off from San Juan, Puerto Rico. Ian noticed that one engine indicated a dangerously high temperature. The crew circled and returned to San Juan. The engine needed replacing. The new one, strapped to an extra wing pod of another B-707, would not arrive until the following day. This meant the crew had to stay overnight in Puerto Rico. That evening, Ian enjoyed a four-course meal and Alpine décor at the *Swiss Châlet*. Not the style of hotel he had expected in San Juan. (The hotel has since been demolished.) Except for what Ian had seen in movies and photographs, he knew little about Swiss architecture and décor. The dining room had wooden beams, cuckoo clocks, wall paintings of past heroic Swiss battles, and *Wilhelm Tell*, the legendary folk hero. Swiss delicacies were served on checkered tablecloths. The hotel's owner had made an agreement with Pan American to include meals for overnighting crews. They could choose anything from the menu: fondue, *rösti* potatoes, veal in

Swiss châlet.

a cream sauce. All were new to Ian. He thought he'd entered a gourmet's paradise. It was the first of many gastronomical feasts that Ian enjoyed during his career with Pan American. Crewmembers usually dressed for these occasions. Smart casual did not exist. On a subsequent layover in Buenos Aires, the entire crew of pilots and stewardesses gathered in the hotel's lobby before going to a restaurant. Ian appeared in a golf shirt. His captain took one look at Ian and asked if he had anything better to wear. Ian said he did not, and the captain told him to go back to his room. Pan American pilots represented the airline even when off-duty and were expected to dress in jacket and tie. Ian never made that mistake again. He was proud to be a member of the Pan American family, given its famous name and global route structure. It was a world of glamor that Ian Duncan could not have imagined as a young lad in Butler, Pennsylvania.

At year's end, on December 30th, 1964, Ian left New York on Pan American's renowned flight *Two*. He flew around the globe to Tokyo and returned westbound on flight *One*. *Clippers One* and *Two* flew continuously around the world in both directions. (Pan American's call sign for air traffic control was clipper, a reference to the 19th century merchant sailing vessels.) Clipper Two departed New York for London, Frankfurt, Vienna, Istanbul, Beirut, Tehran, Karachi, New Delhi, Calcutta, Rangoon, Bangkok, Hong Kong, Saigon, Tokyo, Honolulu, and San Francisco. Clipper One went the opposite direction from San Francisco and eventually ended in New York. Not all cities were on a daily schedule, and landing depended on the day of the week. In the middle of the night somewhere between India and Thailand, both flights passed each other at 1,200 miles per hour. Pan American pilots listened to air traffic control (ATC) clearance of Clipper One and Two, calculated the point of meeting, then greeted each other on the Pan Am radio frequency. This was also a chance for lovers to throw a kiss over the air waves. Years later, when Ian and I were flying around the world, I would be summoned to the cockpit so Ian could hear my voice as he passed by at 36,000 feet.

On January 7th in 1965, Ian was on his return westbound from Bangkok to Beirut on a flight he would not forget. After a brief stopover in New Delhi, the crew continued to their next destination, Tehran. Half-way into the three-hour flight, they learned that Tehran was forecasting snow with potential accumulation on a slippery runway. The option was to continue an additional two hours to Beirut, the alternate airport. But passengers were waiting to board in Tehran, which meant the crew would make every effort to land. Ian kept close check on fuel while the plane spent thirty minutes in a holding pattern. But conditions did not improve. The only choice was to continue on to Beirut. With a headwind forecast at 30-40 knots, Ian felt confident they could reach Beirut with enough fuel to spare, even with a missed approach. Instead, the headwind turned out to be 60-80 knots, double the forecast at all altitude levels. Fuel became critical. The crew discussed landing in Damascus, Syria, then a Pan American station and east of Beirut, across the Anti-Lebanon Mountains.

The captain faced a dilemma. They were 20 minutes from Damascus, when he decided to head straight for Beirut, because the weather showed a clear and sunny sky for their arrival that morning. Ninety miles east of Beirut, Ian noted 3000 pounds of remaining fuel. The captain asked ATC for priority landing. This meant all other flights had to stay away until *Clipper One* was safely on the ground. To conserve fuel, the crew opted for a high level altitude descent. After crossing the mountains into Lebanon at 10,000 feet, they went to idle thrust, applied all available drag: full flaps, landing gear down. Ian cautioned the captain against speed brakes, which with full flaps was not advisable. The captain ignored Ian's advice. Flying at 190 knots (speed limitation for full flaps) the aircraft shook and rattled as it descended 3000 feet a minute. Ian made an announcement over the PA system: "Beirut air traffic control asked us to make a quick descent. There's nothing to worry about. Just remain seated." The no-smoking light came on, usually a sign for stewardesses to secure galleys and get to their jump seats. The plane leveled off at 1500 feet and circled out over the Mediterranean for a final approach. By then all low-level fuel warning lights were blinking. Ian connected the fuel tanks on the manifolds for use in each engine. With an urgency, he told the captain, "You better land!" With 2000 pounds of fuel, there was hardly enough for a go-around if he missed the approach. The low-fuel warning lights continued blinking all the way to the gate. In his logbook, Ian recorded the flight time from New Delhi: seven hours, twenty minutes. This was two hours longer than planned. In retrospect, Ian said they should have landed in Damascus.

On the ground, Ian asked the maintenance supervisor to dip-stick the tanks. Had the fuel gauges been right? What was the actual amount? The supervisor determined 1500 pounds of remaining fuel, hardly enough for a missed approach and go-around. A close call. During his remaining months as a flight engineer, Ian developed a strong objection to stretching the amount of fuel. In planes of that era, gauges were often faulty and inaccurate. "Big planes don't glide well when out of fuel. Not a chance anyone should take," Ian told me.

While in Beirut, Ian arranged to meet Saoud Salaam, his 1952 roommate from the Spartan School of Aeronautics. Saoud had become a pilot for Middle East Airlines, initially flew Vickers Viscounts before becoming a captain on their Sud Aviation SE 210 Caravelle. Ian had maintained occasional contact with Saoud, a card now and then, addressed to Captain Saoud Salaam, Middle East Airlines, New York. Now in Beirut, Ian phoned Saoud, asked to join him for dinner. That evening, the two friends re-visited the past while sharing a *mezze*, a lengthy Lebanese feast with a multitude of small dishes, a new phase of Ian's gastronomical adventures. They concluded the evening by watching belly dancers in the bar of the Intercontinental Hotel. The following day, Ian flew back to Tokyo with layovers in Calcutta and Bangkok.

Years later, flying for Pan American, I became acquainted with Saoud and his wonderful family. His uncle was the Prime Minister of Lebanon, a brother, the president of Middle East Airlines. We visited Lebanon's ski resorts, admired the historic city of Baalbek

Saoud and Ian in front of the Temple of Bacchus in Baalbek, Lebanon, 1971.

in the Beqaa Valley, enjoyed a picnic at Saoud's beach house. I fell in love with Lebanese hospitality and *joie de vivre*. But then civil war broke out, and Beirut was never again the same.

Two and a half months after that risky landing in Beirut, Ian left again on a round-the-world flight. His flight patterns often varied from the schedules of captains and co-pilots. An onboard relief pilot allowed for rest periods and longer duty hours. But there was no relief for the lone flight engineer. For that reason, Ian disembarked alone in Karachi on April 1st, 1965, for a three-day layover. The cabin crew also stayed with the plane. Ian soon learned that Pan American pilots had gone on strike; that another clipper would not be landing in three days; that he would be left stranded in Pakistan. Although he stayed at the modern Intercontinental Hotel, a massive rectangular landmark overlooking the city, feasted on *Tikka* kebabs and savory chicken dishes at the hotel's well-known dining room, he missed the companionship of other crew members. Pan American's station manager felt sorry for Ian, showed him around town, took him for a boat ride, and invited him to his home for a family dinner. Then on day six, Ian answered a call to his room. He was told to get to the lobby at once. Ian rushed down and there stood an official in a Pakistani military uniform. The man told Ian that he had entered Pakistan on a 72-hour crewmember's visa and overstayed his visit by several days. What is your airline's intention, the official demanded? Are you being left here? Are you going to apply for a visa based on emergency? Ian said he didn't know the details and called the station manager, who rushed to the hotel. The trio left for the visa office and waited there. Several hours went by. Ian assumed there was only one reason for the Pakistani government to keep track of him. They thought he was a spy. He would never know but was given an extended visa. The strike went on for another three days, and it took time for all flights to resume their schedules. The first westbound Clipper One landed in Karachi on April 13th. That day Ian flew on to Beirut, Istanbul, Vienna, and Frankfurt. On the 14th he returned to the United States. W. Northacker, the chief flight engineer of Pan American's Internal German Service (IGS), was an extra crewmember on that flight from Frankfurt to JFK. He was impressed with Ian's performance and wrote a letter to the chief flight engineer at JFK, which included these words. "Mr. Duncan is highly motivated to perform in the manner he has been instructed. He also was interested in providing me with helpful hints in tracking fuel and in the operation of the vapor cycle air condition. He is indeed a credit to the organization."

On August 22nd, 1965, Ian flew as a flight engineer from New York to Bermuda and back, his last flight in that position. Two days later, he received his air transport pilot certificate and type rating for the Boeing 707. At the time, there was no B-707 simulator. All training and check-rides were done in the aircraft, either at Grumman Peconic River Airport near Riverhead, New York, or at Atlantic City Airport, New Jersey. Ian demonstrated to an FAA designated instructor pilot how to execute slow flight, steep turns, emergency descent, one and two engines-out-approaches. He landed the aircraft with flaps full, flaps down, and during a crosswind. Another tricky maneuver at higher altitudes in the early B-707 was a recovery from the Dutch roll, a combination of yawing and rolling oscillations. (The roll mode is so named because the plane's recovery motion resembles the rhythmical flow of a Dutch skater on a frozen canal.) After a four-hour-check ride, Ian was qualified to fly left or right-seat on the Boeing 707. But he still had to complete a long-range navigator test.

In 1965, the FAA had approved Pan American's proposal to eliminate the navigator position from their crew requirement. Until then, long range flights over water required a licensed navigator (who was also a pilot). He sat in the rear of the cockpit and faced a panel with a compass and a Loran set. The navigator also took celestial readings with a sextant. To do so, he inserted the periscope of a sextant through a shutter mount in the cockpit's ceiling. Not easy for someone shorter than

6-feet, 4-inches tall. Most navigators stood on a small box. Since this type of navigation was only required for flights over water, the navigator disembarked at the first stop after the plane crossed the Atlantic or Pacific. To eliminate the position, the airline had to install a Loran set on a pedestal between captain and co-pilot and qualify all co-pilots as navigators. Once the navigator's position became obsolete, his chair in the cockpit served as a rest seat for stewardesses, or to accommodate an occasional 'pass rider'.

On September 4th, a week after his B-707 'type rating', Ian passed his navigation check on Pan American's flight 114 from New York to Paris and became a first officer, as co-pilots were known on Pan American. Not until 1978 did his seniority allow him to become a captain. As a first officer on the B-707, and later flying the B-747, he received the paycheck he had hoped for when he left the military. And with an average monthly schedule of 73 flight hours, he had many free days to continue flying in the New York Air National Guard.

15

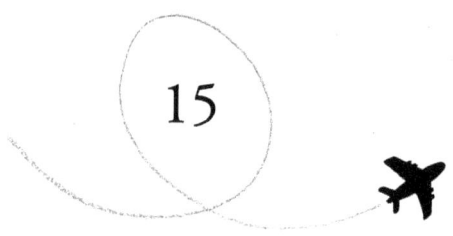

In 1964, the year Ian began his career with Pan American, he commuted from his New Jersey home to JFK Airport. His route led past Floyd Bennett Field, a New York Air National Guard (ANG) base in Brooklyn along the Jamaica Bay shore. One day, the C-97 aircraft on the ramp caught his attention. Could there be an opportunity to fly the plane he knew so well? On a subsequent trip to JFK, he allowed for extra time, drove to Floyd Bennett's gate, and asked to be directed to the base commander.

Inaugurated in 1930, Floyd Bennett Field is named after the man who in 1926, along with Richard Byrd, made the first flight over the North Pole. As New York's first municipal airport, it never achieved commercial interest except for an American Airlines shuttle to Boston. The Midtown Tunnel and the Triborough Bridge were yet to be built, which made Floyd Bennett Field too distant from Manhattan. Airmail traffic went through Newark, New Jersey, accessible via the Holland Tunnel. Floyd Bennett, however, became a desirable field for general aviation. It attracted famous aviators and was the origin and destination of record-breaking flights. A rumored story for new flight personnel was that a panel near the terminal's front desk had an engraved heart, pierced with an arrow, and the inscription Charles Lindbergh loved Amelia Earhart. Ian never found it!

That day in 1964, the ANG's commander said the unit would be fortunate to have someone with Ian's experience. After a check-ride on December 14th, Ian became a C-97 commander, instructor pilot, and flight examiner in the 102nd air transport squadron.

Why did Ian stay in the ANG? Most of Ian's former Air Force buddies left the military after they joined a major airline. What purpose was there for drill weekends and military exercises when Pan American, known as the world's most experienced airline, guaranteed security and sufficient income? Ian had several reasons. He liked flying the C-97, wanted to further his military career, and contribute to the Vietnam War effort. And after his 1972 costly divorce, Ian flew in the ANG to supplement his income.

The 102nd squadron at Floyd Bennett Field supported the Military Airlift Command. Ian flew cargo to U.S. military bases in Germany, England, and Spain. He transported soldiers home on leave, and from 1966 onward, flew ammunition into Vietnam. Although Pan American was obligated to grant a leave of absence for military assignments, Ian never requested one. He welcomed both paychecks and fit missions into his airline schedule.

A roundtrip to Vietnam via Honolulu, Wake Island, Guam, and the Philippines took ten days. Heavy crates of mortar shells and grenades lined the C-97's fuselage. On occasion a soldier, who had been home on emergency leave, was aboard. Ian would land at Da Nang, Cam Ranh Bay, and Saigon. The C-97 never spent more than three hours on the ground before returning to Clark Air Base or Cubi Point Naval Air Station in Manila. The aircraft held enough fuel for the six-hour round-trip.

While approaching Vietnamese territory, Ian hoped for cloudy conditions to elude the occasional sniper near the airfields. At 10,000 feet or higher, he applied the C-97's full drag and made a spiraling rapid descent. When caskets replaced the cargo, the mission was grim. Without medical staff onboard, the crew was unqualified to transport wounded soldiers. Ian recalls deep sadness as he walked through a cabin lined with caskets, each showing name, rank, and date of birth. Was his country's involvement in Vietnam worth the price of so many young men? Ian did not dwell on the political reality and accepted the mission as bringing the deceased home. At Tachikawa Air Base, Japan, the cadavers underwent mortuary protocol before being shipped to Dover Air Force Base in Delaware for release to their families.

Timetables in and out of Vietnam varied. In order not to miss his next Pan American flight, Ian scheduled two free days upon his return. In the winter of 1967, he was glad for this. A snowstorm was predicted for the northeastern United States. Already a day late, Ian had requested extra fuel before departing Travis AFB in California. His alternate airport was Columbus, Ohio. A few hours into the flight, Floyd Bennett Flight Operations advised Ian via Air Traffic Control (ATC) that snow accumulation could force closure by midafternoon. He was near Harrisburg, Pennsylvania when ATC informed Ian that Floyd Bennett would shut down within the hour. Ian was not sure if the closure meant Floyd Bennett Naval Air Station, which controlled Flight Operations, or its tenant, the Air National Guard. ATC confirmed the latter would close between 4 and 5 p.m. After a discussion with his crew, Ian made the decision to touch down in snow at Floyd Bennett. If the runway was icy, he would apply full power, take off immediately, and divert to Columbus.

As the plane began its descent, ATC advised that the current weather was 400 feet overcast, half a mile visibility, with snow showers. Runway conditions, the main factor for closing the base, were not reported. Communications ceased until the flight was on ground- controlled approach for landing. As the C-97 broke out of clouds at 400 feet, the runway was in sight. But its light markers, frosted with ice, were barely visible. The plane touched down in 4-6 inches of snow, enough to slow it down with little reverse thrust. Ian thanked the ground controller for his guided approach and asked that he close the flight plan. A blue pick-up truck, lights flashing, appeared at the runway's turn-off point to guide the C-97 to a parking spot.

When the crew entered the building, the Flight Operation's director applauded them. Until informed the C-97 was inbound, the director had felt certain Ian would divert to Ohio. He knew the ANG's commanding general would be relieved to know that his son, Ian's flight navigator, was safely home. The following morning, Major Markowitz, the full time technician and operations officer, called Ian at home. Ian recalls the major's irritated tone of voice. "Duncan," he said, "I don't appreciate all the extra work. Don't you understand that we have to clear the plane of snow and ice before moving it into the hangar?" Ian knew the words were in jest. He countered that he would be happy to help but that afternoon had a Pan American flight to Frankfurt. Markowitz laughed, "Duncan, you're the biggest disappearing act I know."

All C-97 pilots at Floyd Bennet flew for an airline. They were a friendly bunch who enjoyed camaraderie over a beer, in particular at 4 p.m., after a drill weekend. Officers and NCOs gathered at the clubhouse, an old building on base near the terminal. On one occasion, some of the grown men turned juvenile. The party was breaking up, and three Eastern Airlines pilots were the first to leave. They got into their cars, each one an old clunker of little value, used for airport commuting. The first guy accidently backed into the car behind him. Pilot number two drove over and hit the first guy's front fender. By then Ian and others had exited the club, stood outside, and watched the spectacle unfold. Others went to their cars and joined the melee. Fender benders turned into car bashing, the drivers crashing into each other from all sides. The commanding officer turned up and got into the middle of the scene, ordered a "cease and desist," and sent everyone home. Apparently, the cars were still drivable.

Today Ian regards the event as humorous in retrospect. A momentary surge of built-up animosity among male egos! The commander ordered everyone in the unit, and no excuses, to attend a briefing at 8:30 a.m. on the following drill weekend. He chastised the men involved and called them immature teenagers. And should there be a recurrence, they would be dismissed from the unit. As far as Ian knows, the incident was not mentioned again.

In September 1969, the Air National Guard unit at Floyd Bennett converted to an air refueling squadron. Fighter units in the northeastern United States required tanker practice. Training with Air Force KC-135 tankers was limited because SAC needed them to refuel SAC bombers. Ian's good fortune was his years of experience in the KC-97. Now he would be flying the newer version, the KC-97L, which had more sophisticated radar equipment and could carry 85,000 pounds of fuel. An extra jet engine mounted under each wing increased the KC-97L's power, so it could refuel fighters at 220-230 knots without tobogganing. A central command coordinated all practice flights within a 4000-feet altitude sector, blocked from airline traffic. The plane carried Avgas to power its radial piston engines, plus jet fuel for its two jet engines, and for offloading to the fighters.

Ian enjoyed being a tanker pilot again. He said after years of flying the KC-97 and C-97, the plane fit him like a glove. He knew every niche, knew its weaknesses and strengths, could lead his crew through all situations and weather. Yet he never became overconfident. A pilot's nemesis, as he calls it. In February 1970, Ian, by then Major Duncan, became commander, instructor pilot,

Boeing KC-97L

and flight examiner on the KC-97L.

Four months later, in June 1970, the Department of Defense closed Floyd Bennett Field. The Navy offloaded the property, and its tenant, the Air National Guard, had to leave. The squadron, together with the group and wing, moved to Suffolk County Airport, now Francis S. Gabreski Airport, near Westhampton Beach on Long Island. For personnel living in Brooklyn, it was a long commute. The National Park Service acquired most of Floyd Bennett's terrain. A small helicopter group for Coast Guard and New York City police remained, and a Marine Corps Reserve Unit moved in. By the century's end, New York's Department of Sanitation used the old runway for truck-driving practice; and since 2003, a 119-foot-tall Doppler radar tower records wind shears for use at nearby JFK Airport.

At Suffolk County Airport, Ian continued flying tanker missions, soon earned the rank of Lt. Colonel, became the squadron's Air Operations Officer, and the group's Safety Officer. By the end of 1972, the KC-97s were taken out of service, and the 102nd transitioned to a fighter-interceptor squadron. Ninety percent of its personnel, pilots, navigators were sent elsewhere. The Great Falls Air National Guard in Montana dispatched their F-102s to Suffolk. F-102 pilots, mostly Vietnam veterans, transferred in. Two T-Birds (T-33) joined the group. Lt. Col. Saddlemire, an American Airlines pilot and former C-97 pilot at Floyd Bennett Field, became the 102nd squadron's commander. Ian was its operations officer. Neither was qualified in fighters but both pilots were trained to fly the T-33.

Ian flew the T-33 as a live radar target for the F-102s. No one occupied the backseat on these missions. Air Defense Control gave a steady heading and altitude, then controlled the F-102s into the targeting range to shoot a radar beam at the T-33. As a countermeasure, the T-33 carried chaff dispensers under its wings. With a rotary switch, Ian could release large bunches of foil chaff, which consisted of tiny aluminum strips. These metallic clouds cluttered the F-102's radar, thus permitting the T-33's escape. Ian, nonetheless, was hit hundreds of times. He also had ways to enliven the scene. With a grin he told me about rapid descents and steep climbs, quick turns from left to right. The T-33 had to be flown manually, which obviously delighted him. Tom and Jerry, William Hanna's cat and mouse cartoon characters, and their perpetual chase, came to my mind, and I laughed. Ian wanted to know what was so funny. "You were like Jerry, the elusive mouse." The comparison was not appreciated!

Lockheed-T-33

Some missions meant Ian flew into Canadian airspace to mock intercept with the Canadian Air Force over Nova Scotia and Quebec in order to test their radar. Other drills were held on the southern border. This brought to mind a memory. In the fall of 1973, I had hoped to spend a few days in Key West with Ian. We were still unmarried but living together then, and our flight schedules rarely placed us home at the same time. Ian had orders to fly a T-33 from New York to Key West and participate in nightly radar avoidance exercises. I travelled on Eastern Airlines, upon arrival rented a car, checked into a motel, then drove to Key West's Naval Air Station. At that time, there was no gate or sentry to check an ID card. I parked in front of a building by the runaway, walked into base operations, and asked for Lt. Col. Duncan's arrival time. A young officer said, "No more flights today."

"Are you sure?" I felt my stomach churn.

"Yes, Ma'am. Sure."

I walked out in a panic. What to do? I had no way to communicate with Ian. Back at the motel, I called Suffolk County Air National Guard, heard that Ian's flight had left hours earlier. They could not tell me his whereabouts. I felt alarm, feared there had been an accident. Anxiously I dialed the operator for directory assistance and wrote down phone numbers for every Air Force Base along the Atlantic coast. Eventually I reached someone at Seymour Johnson Air Force Base in North Carolina. I was told Ian had been there. His plane had incurred a mechanical failure, but he was airborne and en route to Key West. Greatly relieved, I hurried back to the Naval Air Station. It was dark outside when I entered base operations. The junior officer I'd met earlier was closing up. He told me to go home.

"No. My boyfriend is arriving in a T-33."

The young man shook his head. "No more flights today."

"You better check again," and told him what I'd heard from Seymour Johnson. My emphatic tone of voice worked. He picked up a phone and spoke to Air Traffic Control. Shortly thereafter, Ian landed and walked in. The junior officer saluted Ian, said he was a lucky guy, that a determined young lady was waiting for him.

In 1974, during a week on temporary active duty, weather and mechanical problems left him grounded for three days. For lack of any other activity, the duty officer assigned Ian to visit a Catholic orphanage and school near Suffolk County Airport and talk about the ANG. The 102nd fighter squadron expected officers and airmen to participate in community affairs in order to gain political support in Congress. The morning of the visit, Ian dressed in a flight suit. He was certain the sage green, full-body garment with his squadron's colorful patch, its winged name tag, and multiple zippered pockets would intrigue the children more than his Air Force uniform. On the way to the school, he stopped at a convenience store for lollipops. Characteristic of Ian's flair for amusing an audience, he let the third and fourth graders check the suit's pockets. Out came pencils, a chart, handkerchiefs, Nomex gloves, a flashlight, and lollipops. One of the youngsters asked why all the pockets were in front, on his chest, arms and legs, but none on his back. Ian told the boy to imagine being strapped tightly to a cockpit seat. Could he reach a back pocket? He shook his head, which

Both photos show Ian at the orphanage.

prompted laughter. That's why, Ian said, a flight suit has no back pockets.

Having their full attention, he spoke about the marvels of flying big airplanes and the importance of learning. He assured the well-behaved youngsters that, regardless of their race and background, they could achieve anything if they studied and did well in school.

The HC-130 "Hercules" and the HH-60G Pave Hawk helicopter refueling over Montauk Point. (Courtesy Photo: USAF ANG 106)

The last aircraft Ian flew in the Air National Guard was the HC-130 Hercules. By 1975, the unit lost its fighters and converted to an air rescue and recovery squadron. Fighter pilots left to join other ANG units. The squadron took in former Air Force C-130 pilots and recruited helicopter pilots to fly the HH-60G Pave Hawks. Ian was included in that conversion and went to C-130 school at Seymour Johnson AFB in North Carolina. To refuel the helicopters, the C-130 extended a probe and drogue system from its outer wing. A capsule with a hose and umbrella held the receptacle for the helicopter.

Ian flew many night-refueling missions. He never forgot one in 1976, nor have I. We'd been married over two years, owned a small house on Long Island. I usually stayed up until Ian came home to serve him a snack. That night, when he walked in, I saw a distressed look on his face. He poured himself a large Scotch, said he was not hungry, and sat at the kitchen table. For Ian to lose his appetite, something awful must have occurred. I asked what had happened.

"Came close to an inflight collision."

Shocked to hear this, I sat down. Ian said he had been flying two miles off Long Island's shore at 105 knots, the required speed for refueling. The helicopter had to descend to reach that speed, intercept the C-130, and attach to the refueling drogue. But the student helicopter pilot came in too fast, higher than he should have. A crewmember, the scanner who watches the join-up from the C-130's window and communicates the progress to both the helicopter and C-130 pilot, yelled over the radio, "Breakaway, breakaway, breakaway," which meant a collision was eminent. Ian applied full power and, shaking in a stall, the C-130 went straight up. In spite of the C-130's loud droning engines, Ian heard the helicopter's blades whirling below. They were *that* close. He poured another Scotch, said that both aircraft returned to base. I could not sit still any longer, got up and paced, finally said, "You could have been killed tonight. Why are you still doing this?"

Ian shook his head, mentally and physically exhausted. He did not know why. Half a fifth of Scotch later, he gave an answer and promised to leave the Air National Guard.

Ian retired the first of December 1976. With his prior service in the Air Force, Ian had served 22 years and flown nine different aircraft: Piper PA-18, North American T-6, North American B-25, Fairchild C-119, Boeing KC-97 (D E F and G versions), Boeing C-97 and KC-97L, Lockheed T-33, Lockheed HC-130 Hercules. He loved each one. But the fully aerobatic, sturdy North American T-6, he had flown at Malden in 1954, remained his favorite.

16

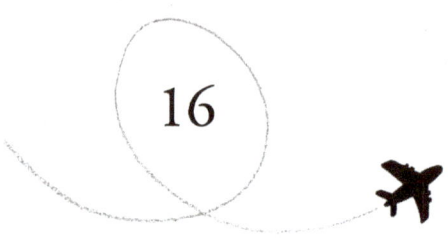

In 1965, as a junior first officer on Pan American's seniority list, Ian flew his first jet aircraft, the Boeing 707. Heavier and longer, with a greater wingspan and more wheels, the plane under normal wind conditions flew eight nautical miles per minute, double the speed of piston aircraft. I asked Ian if he had liked flying the B-707. Had it been more difficult? Ian said the plane was easy to fly. The challenge was landing at foreign airports, initiated during the Second World War. Few were meant to accommodate jets. Narrow taxiways, no central fuel feed, radio beacons, landmarks

Boeing 707.

in unfamiliar languages, and often a single runway to serve a makeshift terminal.

Based in New York, Ian flew to Europe, South America, Africa, Asia, and the Caribbean. Flight crews bid on monthly schedules (bidlines) awarded by seniority. Pilots who wanted to be at home every night, bid daytrips to the Caribbean islands. A commuter from Montana might prefer two 10-day trips, back-to-back. Some crewmembers disliked flying on weekends and holidays, while others preferred a specific destination. Bidlines covered all possibilities. Pilots marked their selections on a bid card, mailed it to scheduling or dropped it in a box at the airport. On large wall rosters schedulers kept track of pilots and cabin crews. Each entry was hand-written and updated daily. Flights that became available due to illness, excessive hours, or a delay returning home, were placed on a recorded phone message for others to grab. As to future revisions, schedulers called crewmembers at home. Those, who had already departed, received a message in-flight or at their hotel. "Be prepared for the latest pattern change," was a common remark among flight crews. This meant to not leave home without beach attire or a sweater.

Many of the B-707 captains, who flew with Ian, had begun their career on Pan American's flying boats. They had fascinating stories to tell. Bob Fordyce was one of them. On a two-week mission, he and Ian were flying cargo around the Pacific. Bob recounted mooring the flying boats, described opening the hatch in the bow, and tossing out a rope with a hook attached to it over to a dock. Often, strong winds and tides pushed the boats in all directions, and hooks missed their targets. Flying boats had no reverse pitch, thrust, or rudders. This meant their captains had to swing them around for a second or third approach. Even decades later, Ian discovered that in Honolulu, Guam, Manila, Wake Island and Okinawa, someone knew Bob as a flying boat officer.

Ian also recalled Jack Burn, a light-weight boxing champion in his youth. Once, when a drunken soldier became unruly on a New York to Frankfurt flight, Jack knocked him out and used seatbelt extensions to bind him to the seatback. Yet Jack's biggest claim to fame was surviving a 1943 flying boat crash into Lisbon's Tagus River. Though severely injured, he rescued Jane Froman, a well-known singer, whom he later married. Ian also told me about Charlie Blair, known for his historic flight in a P-51 over the North Pole from London to San Francisco. Charlie was married to Maureen O'Hara, the legendary film star. She never let her husband out of sight and, until his retirement in 1969, she sat with him in the cockpit. In the late 1960s, most former flying boat pilots reached retirement age. A celebration with champagne honored a captain's last flight and farewell arrival.

Ian's parents basked in their son's successful career and appeared to value it more than his sisters' graduate degrees. Isabella's friends from The Daughters of the British Empire, an American society of British-born women, heard of her international Pan American pilot. Ian even made the news in the *Butler Eagle* newspaper. Isabella liked to show off Ian's gifts: pistachios from Tehran, leather gloves from Rome, Indian jewelry, and German

Hummel figurines. On a globe in their living room, George and Isabella followed their son's travels and awaited his phone calls. Where had he been recently? Who had he met? Had he eaten well? They heard all about Pan American's *haute cuisine*, catered by Maxim's of Paris. Ian told them how he could choose from a first-class menu, food he had not tasted before: Filet of beef, pheasant, veal steak "Maxim," scallops, Dover sole on the lunch or dinner menu. He also learned the pay-off for being attentive to the cabin crew. A stewardess might serve leftover caviar, pâté, smoked salmon, French cheeses, and desserts to those in the cockpit. A favorite of Ian's was *Cannelloni al Forno*, meat-filled pasta rolls in a tomato and béchamel sauce, topped with cheese. This dish, a second meal on Rome to New York flights, was served in tourist class prior to arrival. Such epicurean delights reminded his mother of T.W Phillips' grandiose entertainment events. His father's reaction: "Ye'r living heich oan th' hog mah laddie."

Ian enjoyed telling his parents about Elizabeth Taylor and Richard Burton, who had booked the entire first-class cabin on a flight from New York to Rome. The captain invited the famous actors to the cockpit. In the early morning hours as the plane passed over the west coast of France, Elizabeth sat in the jump seat behind the captain. Ian never forgot her striking, bluish-purple eyes. Surprisingly, she wore little makeup. Richard did not stay long, said he had to finish some reading, and returned to the cabin. Elizabeth was chatty, inquired about the various instruments, seemed interested in every aspect of flying. Would she be allowed to remain in the cockpit for landing? The flight engineer said there was a prerequisite. Prior to descent, she would have to massage the captain's back. She began doing so at once. Before disembarking, she and Richard invited the entire crew to tour the Cinecittà studios and have lunch. Ian, tired after a long night flight, felt he had to decline the invitation.

George and Isabella also heard about Charles Lindbergh, who had been on Ian's flight to Paris. Before departing New York, a boarding agent advised the crew that Col. Lindbergh was onboard in tourist class, row 10. Not wanting to draw attention, Lindbergh travelled incognito and never in first class. For privacy, the seats next to him were blocked. Ian's captain asked a stewardess to hand Lindbergh his business card, inviting him to the cockpit. He arrived shortly thereafter. A quiet, friendly man, joking was not Lindbergh's style. Asked why he was flying to Paris, Lindbergh said he had been invited to give a speech at the Paris Airshow. Ian wanted Lindbergh to know where he grew up. Did he remember landing the *Spirit of St. Louis* at Bettis Field near Pittsburgh in 1927? Lindbergh did remember, said he'd come from Cleveland that day. He recalled the motorcade, the confetti, crowds of people, and a festive banquet that night. When Ian later shared the encounter with his father, George said he would pass this on to Mr. Scholter, who liked to reminisce about meeting Lindbergh in 1927.

Ian's glamorous lifestyle pleased him. As a fifteen-year-old hangar boy at Butler-Graham Field, that was what he had hoped for and now relished his success. Healthy and fit, Ian always passed his required bi-annual physical at JFK airport, where Pan American had a medical office with a small staff of doctors and nurses. They also gave vaccinations: yellow fever, smallpox, typhoid, tetanus, and bi-annual cholera. These were recorded in Pan American's required booklet. The office also issued malaria pills.

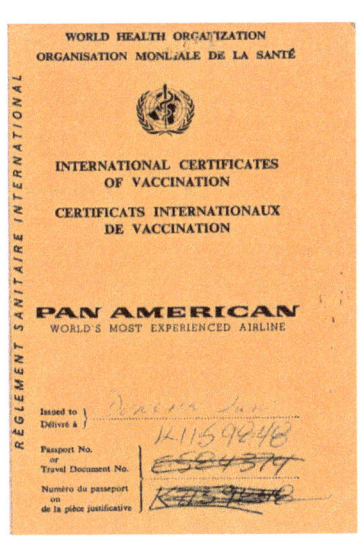

Although I had been a Pan American stewardess since the spring of 1968, I had yet to meet Ian and would not hear until later about what happened to him in 1969. Like all commercial pilots, Ian had to pass an annual first-class physical issued by a Federal Aviation Administration (FAA) appointed physician. During an appointment on March 27th, 1969, the FAA doctor noticed a small wart on Ian's upper right arm and asked how long it had been there. Ian was not sure. He said it had bothered him recently and bled when in contact with his long-sleeved, heavily starched, uniform shirt. Because the wart looked suspicious, the doctor took a biopsy and sent it to a lab for analysis. Two days later, Ian was ordered to return to the office. The doctor looked again at Ian's arm, felt under the armpit, said the small wart was a melanoma. Without delay, Ian was to see a cancer specialist. Unfamiliar with the term melanoma, Ian phoned his sister Isobel, a professor of nursing. She told him that a melanoma was a fast-spreading cancer, one of the worst kinds. In Ian's case, the proximity to the lymph nodes in his armpit made the melanoma particularly dangerous.

Isobel urged him to follow the doctor's recommendation. Ian made an appointment with Dr. Booher, known as the bishop of melanoma surgery at Sloan Kettering in New York. Dr. Booher advised surgery within two days. "How long for the recovery?" Ian asked. Dr. Booher said it depended on how far the melanoma had spread. He would cut away the surrounding tissue, have it tested, then remove more, if necessary, until no further cancer cells remained. "When you come out of anesthesia, Mr. Duncan, look for your right hand." That Ian could lose his arm was unnerving. It would mean the end of his flying career.

The surgery was extensive but successful. No muscle had to be cut. But a 4 by 4-inch skin graft was taken from his right thigh and stitched onto the wound on his arm. Ian spent a week at the hospital, where he met other cancer patients in the dayroom and smoking lounge. Most men were older than Ian. But there were also two teenagers with melanoma. Unfortunately, their outlook was less bright than Ian's whose cancer had not spread.

Pleased with the surgery's outcome, Ian was soon his old jovial self. At the hospital he celebrated with an alcoholic drink before dinner and flirted with the nurses. A tall brunette took a liking to Ian and acted in a coquettish manner. She visited him frequently, took his vital signs longer than was normally done, held on to his hand. One evening she drew the curtains around his bed, said she wanted to make sure all Ian's vital signs were in working order. Ian did not object. He was happy to be alive.

As soon as the graft had healed, Ian squeezed a rubber

ball to exercise the arm. He painted his house and returned to Floyd Bennett to fly the C-97. This time he sat in the right seat to get his right arm ready for flight control. Three months later he passed his FAA physical; and on July 18th, flew his first trip with a check pilot to Frankfurt. For several years he consulted with Dr. Booher. A large scar remained. Ian joked about it. "Want to see where the dog bit me?" People, who didn't know any better, believed him.

Cancer had prompted Ian to reassess his life. Could it be that at thirty-four, he had reached the midpoint of his existence? In months to come, he contemplated ways to spend his remaining years. In a loveless union he felt trapped. Had it not been for his children, he would have left his wife much earlier. They had grown apart, shared no common interests, lived separate lives. Ian was president of the Little League and the Jaycees. He bought a boat and took his boys fishing. David was eleven, Jim nine. His third son, William Scott, born in 1966, was only four years old. Ian loved his children, wanted to care for them and be a good father. How would they react if he moved out, lived somewhere else? For more than a year Ian vacillated. He also wondered how his parents would react. As far as he knew, his divorce would be the first in the Duncan family. What would his father say? Would George admonish Ian for his failed marriage?

At check-in one day, Ian saw an ad on the Pan American bulletin board. A recently divorced captain, Paul Taipale, owned a house in Lynbrook, Long Island. He had a room to let, 75 dollars a month. Ian filled his car with personal belongings, including a brass stand-up lamp. He moved in with Paul, who became a friend for life. Ian's wife immediately sued for divorce. When Ian told his parents he had separated, his father said: "A've bin wondering whit teuk ye sae lang."

On Pan American's flights Ian met young single women with whom he felt compatible, including Dutch, French, British, and Scandinavian stewardesses. One had been Miss Norway. He had no plans to get attached. But now he knew what to expect in a partner.

17

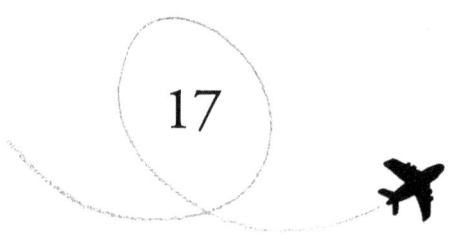

In the summer of 1970, I was part of a cabin crew in the lobby of Rome's Hotel Metropole, awaiting transport to Fiumicino Airport for a flight to Beirut and Tehran. Ian approached and introduced himself as Jim Duncan, said he would be the first officer that day, and shook hands with all six of us. From our first meeting, Ian retained a definite image of me: a smiling young woman with expressive eyes whose high cheekbones framed a beautiful ovular face. I merely recall Ian as tall, polite, and friendly. Later, on the airplane, while preparing for departure, I formed a different opinion. By happenstance, it was my turn that day to work the first-class galley. Had I been in tourist class, Ian could not have requested his coffee, blond and sweet like me. And I doubt anyone else would have spiked his coffee with tabasco, Worcestershire sauce, salt, pepper, and liquid from a jar of olives. That day before take-off, to the amusement of his captain and flight engineer, Ian spit out the nasty coffee and said, "She likes me."

We arrived late that night at the Royal Tehran Hilton, a luxury hotel in the city's northern part at the foothills of the Elburz Mountains. Following the Iranian revolution, the hotel had been renamed the *Parsian Esteghlai* (Persian independence) International Hotel. At 11 p.m., the crew was not ready for sleep, our circadian rhythms not on Tehran's time zone, which was eight hours later than New York. We congregated in the captain's room for drinks and left-over delicacies from the first-class galley. Ian wore dark trousers and a light cashmere turtleneck and looked attractive. But he kept his distance. By 2 a.m. the party broke up, and everyone returned to their rooms.

The following morning, I heard the phone ring. Who could be calling at 10 a.m.? I lifted the receiver and heard, "Jim here. Do you want to come to the bazaar with me?"

I told him I was sleeping and would go later. He asked when I could be ready. I told him early afternoon. He said he would wait. That afternoon, I met him and other crewmembers in the lobby. All of us rode in the hotel's van to the bazaar, a 12-mile distance.

Tehran's Grand Bazaar is a traditional Persian shopping center with mosaics and decorative molding on vaulted ceilings and domes. Hundreds of shops and stalls are within a labyrinth of twisting corridors, each about six miles in length. Vendors sell food, home furnishings, and clothing. Some offered special discounts to Pan American crews and welcomed us with hot tea, served in small traditional glasses. Copper pots and trays were a special bargain. Over time most Pan American crewmembers took home an Iranian copper vessel. Other coveted items were Iranian pistachios, superior in quality, and caviar of the golden variety. Some crewmembers understood that a ten-dollar bottle of Scotch bought at duty-free in Rome could be exchanged for a 300-gram (10.5 ounce) tin of caviar.

On previous occasions I had been to the bazaar, and I did not buy anything that day. After an hour, I was ready to leave. Ian, too. He flagged a taxi and held the door for me. The ride to the hotel took over an hour. Stuck in a traffic jam, we sat in the backseat of a tiny clunker with nothing to do but talk. Ian recalls conversing on subjects long since forgotten. That evening, after dinner with the crew at a Persian restaurant, Ian enticed me with a romantic line. "My balcony has a great view over Tehran. You should see the city's lights." Why not? I thought. While I admired the twinkling lights below, Ian asked for just one kiss. I did not refuse his long, romantic embrace. But in view of a 5 a.m. wake-up call, I returned to my room.

The following evening in Rome, our crew dined near the Spanish steps. After dinner, Ian suggested that he and I walk to the hotel, stop at the Trevi Fountain, and throw a coin to assure that we returned one day. A cool breeze had dispersed the day's blazing heat, and we wandered leisurely through Rome's narrow streets. Back at the hotel, we did not want the day to end, sat at the bar, and discovered commonality in interests outside of work. Three or four glasses of Sambuca later, almost midnight, I said it was time to go upstairs. What I meant was to sleep. Whether on purpose or not, Ian appeared to have misunderstood. "I thought you would never ask," he said. I left his room early in the morning, flew on a non-stop to New York. Ian went to Paris, uncertain if we would meet again. It may seem odd to the reader that we did not exchange phone numbers. I can only surmise that we thought of the encounter as a fleeting passionate moment. Yet Ian could not get me out of his mind. Two weeks later, I discovered a humorous greeting card in my JFK crew mailbox. "I would like to see you again, Jim." He suggested we bid on another flight to Rome and Tehran? And yes, I left a note in his crew mailbox.

In 1970, as a senior first officer, Ian had a good chance for his top choice on bidlines. And because pilots' schedules were awarded before mine, I knew his flights and tried to match them. According to Federal Aviation Regulations, flights to a foreign nation required one stewardess fluent in that country's language. I could speak five. Besides German, my native tongue, I was qualified in Dutch, Russian, French, and Italian. Few Pan American stewardesses spoke Italian, which meant, as a French and Italian speaker, I had super-seniority on Paris/Rome/Tehran flights and usually received my first choice.

Two months later, Ian and I landed back in Rome and began what would be a long, exciting love affair. Each month we compared bidlines to coordinate our flights and, for the following two years, flew to destinations around the world. We walked along the Seine in Paris and the Shannon River in Limerick. At Munich's Octoberfest, we savored beer, bratwurst, even rode a roller-coaster. I watched Ian play golf at Scotland's famous Turnberry Resort, which was also our crew hotel near Prestwick Airport. As tourists in Japan and India, we shopped, dined, and danced. We toured Morocco's souks and watched Kenya's wildlife on safari. If our flights did not coincide, we wrote letters to be kept poste restante at hotels for each other's arrival. Wherever we met, Ian's eyes reflected his joy to be with me. He said I had qualities he had not encountered in other women. Sitting on a beach in Guam, he told me I was perfect.

I warned him that he might be disappointed one day.

Whenever possible, and only on a repositioning flight without people, I sat in the cockpit during take-off or landing and watched Ian at the flight controls. Relaxed in his chair, he controlled the plane in a calm manner, made no abrupt thrust changes, not even during the most horrendous weather conditions and approaches. Except for turbulence, passengers should feel nothing until the plane touched down and the engines went into reverse. A plane ride should be that smooth. This was Ian's motto.

Ian and Ilona, 1972.

One of Ian's superior qualities was his sense of humor. The two of us made full use of it. Play-acting on flights, we pretended we did not know each other, particularly with an unfamiliar crew. I would enter the cockpit to bring a drink or remove a dinner tray. Ian would ask, "Are you inviting me to your room tonight?" I usually snapped back, "Who do you think I am?" Leaving the cockpit, I would mutter, "what a jerk," and bang the door shut. (Cockpit doors were not reinforced then.) But before long, our romance was well-known. Captains offered to trade their larger rooms with Ian. Some crewmembers said our love affair was uplifting, hoped it was contagious. Like a romantic movie, our love story made people dream.

In September 1971, I qualified in Russian so we could fly the Moscow route together: four trips per month, leaving New York every Thursday evening. The flights stopped at Heathrow airport both ways for a crew change. This allowed us time to visit London's museums and in Moscow to go to the *Bolshoi*

Pan Am Aeroflot pin.

Theater. After one month, Ian said his culture-low-level-warning-light was off. I had laughed at his comment and said the following month we would forego Russian opera.

Recently, while recalling the winter of 1972, I asked Ian what he remembered about flying into Soviet airspace. He named old-style radios, limited range of beacons, unclear communications for approaches that required incessant repeating. Then, most countries had pre-set radio frequencies. Not the Soviets. Before entering their airspace, the last controller in Berlin or Copenhagen gave Pan American crews that day's frequency. Russians gave altitude calls in meters, not feet. Even with a conversion chart in the cockpit, converting the constant altitude calls during approach was tedious. Years later, in 2017, Russia transitioned to feet.

During our second stay in Moscow something odd happened. On Sunday morning we packed and were ready to leave the room. Then Ian asked me if I had seen his key ring. It held his house and car keys, plus a cockpit key. One other key was for his personal locker at the Suffolk Country Air National Guard, marked 'property of the U.S. government'. I had last seen the key ring on our dresser where Ian always put small change and keys. We pulled the dresser away from the wall. Nothing there. We checked drawers, looked under the bed, again opened and searched our bags. No keys. Ian reported the loss to the Pan American's station manager. He offered to call the hotel's director and delay the flight. Ian said that was not necessary, as he kept a spare key under his car's bumper at JFK.

Before our next departure, Pan American issued a new cockpit key. A week later, back at Moscow's Metropol Hotel, we were assigned a different room. To our amazement Ian's key ring, all keys included, was on the bedcover. I should not have been surprised. The year before, I had been a language student in Moscow and knew Russian KGB agents kept close watch on me. Obviously, that had not changed.

Pan American's destinations covered cultural diversity, and flights to the Soviet Union were not the only unusual ones. Most of the unconventional flying was in Africa. Pan American crews were pioneers on the continent. The pilots and stewardesses who chose African flights were adventurous. The routes were not easy to fly. Air traffic control and communications were rudimentary, weather forecasts guesswork. Add to this the dangers of malaria, or other diseases from unsanitary conditions.

During the 1960s, only Pan American's DC-8s served the African continent. After they had been sold and replaced by the B-707, Ian began flying the routes. Depending on the day of the week, flights terminated in Nairobi, Dar es Salaam, or Johannesburg, with stops along the way. One of them was Roberts Field Airport in Liberia. Pan American crews knew the putrid smell of stagnant humid air and body odor that awaited them at the Roberts Field terminal.

Built during the Second World War for the Army Air Forces, the field's runway accommodated B-47 Stratojets. Following the war and under contract with Liberia's Ministry of Transport, Pan American was the airport's administrator until 1985. During those years, every Pan American passenger to Africa had to pass through Roberts Field. Crewmembers had three to four-day layovers and stayed at the Roberts Field Hotel, a no-frills establishment in walking distance of the terminal. Dirt roads, jungle, primitive huts surrounded the hotel. But it had a decent restaurant, bar, and pool. The rooms were bare: a simple bed, dresser, small shower, no phone. A bang at the door served as our wake-up call.

During Ian's first lay-over in 1971, he had not known what to expect. On day one he heard banging on the door to his room. "Bus to Caesar's Beach leaves in an hour." Ian put on swim trunks, a hat and shirt, and grabbed a book for the beach. What awaited him were a hotdog stand with beer, and topless stewardesses sunbathing, while others played Frisbee. Ian had not seen topless women in the open air since seeing them from the Phillips' water tower in his youth. And this 'crew' party was private like the gathering at Phillips Hall. Except for Mr. Caesar, crewmembers had the beach to themselves.

On a few occasions, Ian and I were together on African routes, the last time in May 1972. That day we did not arrive on the same flight. I landed from New York in the morning, Ian was due from Nairobi that evening. A party had been planned for the following day. Pilots from Nairobi usually arrived with a side of beef, which the hotel's chef barbequed by the pool. Everyone was invited for food, drinks, and music. Yet on the evening Ian was to land, the sky literally opened up. Thunder, lightning, constant downpour. At the hotel, the consensus among crews was the plane would overfly and continue on to Dakar. I said the first officer, Jim Duncan, would make every effort to get the plane on the ground.

In Accra, Ghana, the plane's last stop, Ian's captain anticipated bad weather and requested extra fuel. It was Ian's turn to fly this segment. For thirty minutes the plane remained in a holding pattern SW of Roberts Field. Only darkness below. During that era, Pan American pilots were allowed to approach African airports with a 'Look-See' attitude. This meant if they saw the runway, they could land. Other destinations prohibited this rule. That night over Roberts Field, the captain asked for a vote. An approach won. During descent, the aircraft bounced up and down, left and right. Rain was so heavy that wipers set to maximum speed barely cleared the windshield. At 400 feet, the runway lights were visible, and the antiskid brakes set to the highest setting. The plane touched down in standing water, which left a wake behind the nose wheel. The engines, in reverse, doused the entire fuselage with water. At the hotel, crewmembers heard the jet's arrival and cheered. With a triumphant smile, I said I knew Jim Duncan would land.

Torrential rain at Roberts Field usually brought land frogs to the runway. They liked to drink fresh rainwater. Ian estimated 10,000 frogs that night, 9000 of which went through the engines. In at the front, out the back. Ground personnel said no wonder the plane's brakes had worked so well, with more frogs under the wheels than water. I wondered about engine damage. According to Ian, the frogs were too soft to cause harm. Jokingly, he said, "They went in whole. Came out fried frog legs!

On June 7th, 1972, Ian flew his last flight as a first officer on the B-707 and began training on the B-747. By then I had cancelled the lease on my Manhattan apartment and moved with Ian to a small furnished house in Long Beach, New York, eleven miles from JFK. The short commute to the airport allowed us to drive each other to and from work. We could only afford one car, a small Chevrolet Vega. It often overheated and conked out.

That summer of 1972, while in training on the B-747, Ian felt the pressure of settling financial arrangements of his divorce, finalized on July 28th. His three sons spent July and August with us. The beach, a short walk from our Long Beach house, meant they could swim in the ocean. To minimize the hours the boys were alone, Ian and I worked out a schedule. Because Ian attended 747 ground school and simulator training, he was home each night. I flew minimum hours to attend to the boys during the day. And because 747 simulators had not yet been approved for full-flight training, Ian had to wait his turn for training in the aircraft. During this interval, Ian flew often for the Air National Guard, took David, Jim, and Scott along, and had them sit by the runway to watch planes take-off and land. Ian remembers it as a long and tiresome summer.

Ian passed his B-747 check ride on September 12th and departed September 18th from New York to London. Five days later, a scary incident occurred on flight One from Beirut to Frankfurt. Shortly after take-off, Beirut station called on the Pan American frequency: "You have a red brick," a code word for bomb. Someone had called the station, said a bomb was on that flight. In the 1970s, hijacking and bomb explosions happened often enough to be taken seriously. Worldwide, there were more than fifty such incidents. A Pan American B-747 was blown up in Cairo September 7th, 1970.

Out of Beirut that morning, the crew dumped fuel and landed. Ian's log shows the flight time was 13 minutes. Passengers disembarked, baggage was removed and inspected. When no bomb was found, the plane took off again. On a later return to Beirut, Ian asked the ground staff what they had discovered about the bomb scare. They said airport and state security teams located the incoming phone number and tracked it to a disconsolate husband whose partner was supposed to be on the flight.

During his long career with Pan American Ian was spared another bomb scare.

People often asked Ian how he felt taking off in this giant plane, which weighs 435,000 to 440,000 pounds, depending on configuration. Add passengers, cargo, fuel, and the B-747 could weigh up to 710,000 pounds, its maximum take-off weight. These are Ian's words: "I would be at the very beginning of the runway, ready to use all the concrete, then power up the four engines, 40,000 pounds of thrust each. Initially, I pushed the throttles up to stabilizing power (50%), slowly adding more thrust. Depending on temperature and pressure altitude, I tried to get maximum power. As the plane moved, I steered with a steerable nose wheel for 20-30 seconds until it reached 80-90 knots of speed and could be steered with the rudder. It's a powerful experience, 160,000-pound-hp engines blowing everything behind you, including lots of fuel – 25,000 pounds per hour."

I asked Ian if he recalled any foolish event during his time as first officer on the B-747. Ian said the most senseless thing happened in October 1975 on a flight from JFK to Frankfurt. One and a half hours after leaving New York, the crew identified an oil leak in one of the engines. The captain, a former flying boat pilot, decided to continue to Gander, Newfoundland. Ian still can't understand why he did not return to JFK, the same distance as Gander. At JFK, there would have been a spare engine, possibly another aircraft, and a fresh crew. Instead, this captain, a moron according to Ian, ordered the engineer to dump fuel, so the aircraft would be at the right landing weight

First Officer Duncan in front of Clipper Great Republic, a B-747 SP, 1976.

at Gander. Pan American had to send a second 747. After minimum crew rest, Ian and his crew continued to Frankfurt. Check airmen flew the three-engine 747 back to New York. In all, a huge expense for the airline.

The B-747's Pratt & Whitney engines were an amazing engineering feat of that era. Plus, they were reliable. During the thirteen years Ian flew the B-747, he only had three occasions to shut down an engine in flight for fear of running low on oil and causing a potential fire.

18

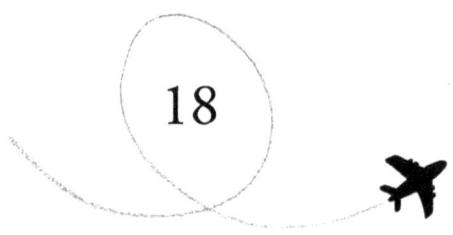

In spring 1972 Ian's sisters welcomed me to the family. I immediately liked Helen and her husband Bob, both lovers of classical music. Helen played piano and the church organ. She taught special education in high school while Bob, a Ph.D. in organic chemistry, worked for the DuPont Corporation. They lived with their three young sons in Glassboro, New Jersey. Ian's sister, Isobel, recently married to Phillip Hartley, an economics professor at Rutgers, lived in a stately home in Morristown, New Jersey.

After meeting Ian's sisters, I noticed that Helen and Isobel called their brother Ian, not Jim. To his nephews he was Uncle Ian. Why did everyone else call him Jim? Ian told me that he had grown tired of correcting people who mispronounced his name *Ee-yan*, *Eye-yan*, and *Jan*. So he called himself Jim, short for James, his middle name. I preferred to call him Ian, as he was known to his family. This also prevented confusion between a father and son with the same name. But, in the airline industry, until his retirement, Ian continued to be known as Jim Duncan.

Isabella and George planned to visit us the fall of October 1972. Ian had praised his parents so often that I arranged my schedule to be home during their stay. To my delight I discovered they liked literature (George a fan of Somerset Maugham) and appreciated classical music. After their visit Isabella wrote me a note, which I kept. "Belated but none the less sincere thanks for your many kindnesses to us when we visited at Long Beach. Your thoughtfulness will not be forgotten. The time seemed to pass quickly, and we enjoyed listening to your records. Your knowledge of good music makes George and me feel like amateurs."

A month later, Ian and I spent Thanksgiving weekend with Helen, Bob, and their sons at their shore house near Cape May. The traditional family gathering, which included Ian's three sons, was my initiation to duck hunting.

Ian and I had made a pact to partake in each other's sports and cultural interests. In the future, I would attend country music events, listen to artists like Willy Nelson and Kris Kristofferson; and Ian would accompany me to opera, concerts, and the theater. And if Ian took me skiing, then I agreed to go fishing and duck hunting.

I will never forget that Thanksgiving morning when Ian led me to a duck blind in New Jersey's salt marshes, a wide inner coastal wetland. Everyone except Helen, who did not hunt and stayed with the younger two boys, got up early and put on gear. My clothes and boots, borrowed from Ian's nephews, were a bad fit, though I hoped they would keep me warm. A short ride in Bob's open boat took us to three blinds, separated by 200 feet. The temperature had been below freezing the night before. Few words were spoken as we sat tightly together, the boat advancing through the calm, mysterious darkness. At the first drop-off point, Ian and

I stepped onto a sandy shore, then walked a short distance across swampy grounds to our blind. I could barely see my feet and my left boot momentarily stuck in the mud. By the time we reached the blind (a square frame covered in burlap and straw), I felt cold wetness inside my boots.

The sun slowly rose above the horizon and exposed a clear, wintry sky. Ian and I sat quietly on milk crates and watched for ducks. The day before, Bob's older boys had placed several decoys around the blind to attract visitors. A pair of high-flyers approached. Ian stood and aimed. But the ducks were too fast and high. Disappointed, he sat down again and lit a cigarette, which he said guaranteed imminent action. We sat there, my feet more painfully cold, and wiggling my toes did not help. I tried marching in place to create warmth. Ian warned me my movements would scare the birds. Back on the milk crate, I quietly suffered. Suddenly, three ducks approached. "Your turn. Get ready," Ian said. I grabbed the gun, pointed it upward, heard "aim, shoot." I pulled the trigger. The gun kicked back, and I felt a sharp pain in my chest. "You got one." Ian said ecstatically. A dead duck almost landed in our blind.

That morning, before we returned to Helen's, Ian shot two more birds. Hardly a catch to justify numb feet and the bruised chest I saw in the shower. Over the following days, the group shot mallards, wigeons, a few black ducks, and buffleheads. Unfortunately, these birds feed on small fish that live in the wetland. This causes their meat to taste fishy. Still, some of the locals liked them and appreciated the donations. Ian asked how they cooked the ducks. "With lots'o sauce!"

After that weekend, I took trap and skeet shooting lessons at a private club north of Manhattan. For Valentine's Ian gave me a Remington 12-gauge 870 shotgun. Before returning for another Thanksgiving at the New Jersey shore, I bought proper boots and hunting gear.

As to skiing, Ian took lessons in Killington, Vermont, home of the gradual-length ski method. Given his height, Ian looked comical on skis the size of a skateboard. Yet he soon graduated to longer skis and joined me on intermediate runs. Traffic on the slopes was Ian's main concern, that another skier could run into him and cause a mid-slope collision. He was a pilot and required traffic control. I told him he was not in the air. "There is no Ski Traffic Control, Ian. Go with the flow." But Ian never outgrew this fear. Yet for years we enjoyed an annual family vacation on the slopes in Stowe, Vermont. Then one day Ian somehow lodged a ski pole in his ribcage and declared his skiing days were over.

Ian remembers 1972 as a good year. The stress of his divorce ended, he was happy with the woman he loved, and flew the B-747. But later in December of that year, he received disturbing news. His father had been admitted to a hospital for exploratory stomach surgery. Worse news followed. The surgeon determined that George had incurable pancreatic cancer and would be sent home. In early January 1973, Ian and I drove to Butler. Isobel was the first to arrive, Helen some days later. Dr. Lucas, the Duncan's family physician, came to the house and explained that George might have six months to live. To ease his pain, he needed Demerol injections. Ian, his sisters, and I agreed to help with his care. We promised that one of us would always be with George and Isabella. Dr. Lucas then demonstrated how to give an injection, which we practiced on an orange.

From Ian's Pan American logbook, I have determined the weeks when Ian did not fly so he could be with his father. Sometimes he drove to Butler, other times he flew to Pittsburgh and rented a car. Ian remembers his father's stalwart nature. George knew his life was ending. Yet he never complained. By May he could not digest regular food and took only liquids: consommé, Jell-O, and applesauce. George was never a large or tall man, 5 foot nine, maybe ten, 150 pounds. Ian recalls his father's gradual weight loss. When he became too weak to stand, Ian lifted him off the bed and carried him to the bathroom. He could not have weighed more than ninety pounds. Yet George remained mentally sharp and grateful to the end. Father and son reminisced about Phillips Hall, recalling humorous and serious episodes. Ian was on the edge of his father's bed one day when George compared their professions. "Tis odd, ah hauled yin fowk aroond, ye carry mony families at wance." (George hauled one family around, Ian flew many at once.)

George Duncan died on June 25th, 1973. He was seventy-two. By chance, Ian and I were home in New York when Isobel called with the news. She said their father died peacefully in bed, next to Isabella, his wife of 44 years. We drove to Butler that same day, went straight to the Thompson Miller Funeral Home, and were with Isobel and her mother to receive friends for visitation that evening. Helen offered to collect Ian's sons and bring them along with her family. The funeral on June 27th was a well-attended event, with music, prayer, and tributes to George. That morning I felt deeply moved when Isabella bent over the open casket, kissed George, and said, "Good bye my love." The family proceeded to the internment at Greenlawn Burial Estate. In 1950, George and Isabella had decided on their burial place, paid for it in advance. Ian and his sisters chose a gravestone marker, which by regulation had to be flat on the ground.

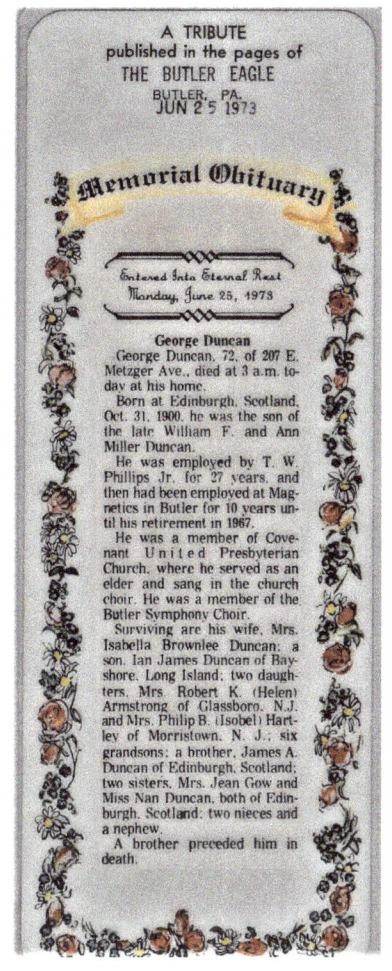

George was Ian's hero, the pillar of the Duncan clan. A quiet man, he seldom raised his voice. But he was not easily intimidated. Raised in a poor section of Edinburgh, he finished school at fourteen, became self-supporting as a print setter, and contributed to the cost of living at home. With his work ethics and good nature, George impressed his boss. The man loaned George the money to immigrate to the United States and improve his standard of living. Ian said his father was well-read and had good penmanship. Unfortunately, his father's letters did not survive. Ian said their contents were always meaningful. Ian remembers George as a happy man who enjoyed what life offered. People liked him, including Mr. Phillips and the staff at Phillips Hall. I liked him, too. A card from Isabella in August 1973 touched me: "A little note of thanks to you from George for the loving care you gave him. He always asked for your backrubs, and I thank you most sincerely for your concern and kindness. As you know, he was very fond of you."

Ian said his father taught him humility, grace, perseverance, and patience. Many nights, crossing the ocean, Ian would observe the stars with his father in mind. In 1923, on a ship from Liverpool, George must have looked at the same stars, wondering what his future held. The spiritual connection to his father never faded, and he remained forever dear in Ian's heart.

Ian with his mother at Greenlawn Burial Estate.

19

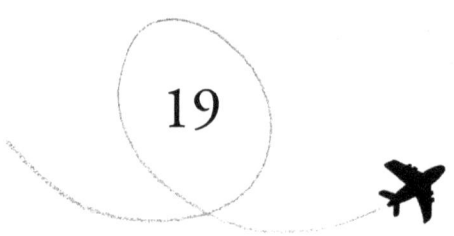

While Ian and I cared for his dying father in the spring of 1973, the lease on our Long Beach residence came up for renewal. Rather than rent, we bought a house in Bayshore, New York. Until closing day, Ian hadn't seen the place. I was to buy whatever I liked as long as we could afford it. My chosen new home, a high ranch house with a swimming pool, was in a blue-collar development. As a down payment, Ian used his VA loan eligibility. When the previous owners finally met Ian, they showed signs of relief. "Thank God," the wife said to her husband. I asked what she meant. She said they could only think of one reason why I had not brought Ian to the house; that he was black. Shocked by this, I preferred not to answer her.

Five months later, in January 1974, the United Services Automobile Association (USAA), our insurance agent, warned that unless we were married, our house insurance would be cancelled. We opted to elope to Las Vegas and were married at the Chapel of the Bells on March 26th. A taxi driver was our witness. That evening, after dinner at a French restaurant, we called our mothers from the hotel. A nine-hour time difference meant it was early morning when my mother lifted the receiver in Germany. In a quavering voice, she congratulated us. But

Ilona and Ian wedding, Las Vegas, 1974.

Isabella Duncan was not pleased, as she would have preferred a proper wedding. And Ian's sisters wished they had been included. Yet ever after, Ian and I agreed that eloping had been our best solution.

After the wedding we flew to Puerto Vallarta, Mexico, and spent a week on the beach. We also rode horses, parasailed, and chartered a fishing boat. Pan American's employee travel office had booked the grand hotel Posada Vallarta, which offered Pan American employees a discount. Despite Ian's airline friends' betting that our marriage would not last three years, we have grown old together.

Later in 1974, Pan American offered a temporary three-week assignment in Tehran. Several B-747 crews were needed to fly pilgrims to Jeddah on their hajj, the obligation Muslims should fulfil once in a lifetime. Iran's Shah Reza Pahlavi funded the entire operation. Apparently, he hoped his generosity would appease the mullahs, who opposed his rule for alleged corruption. Ian and I liked the idea of spending the first weeks of January 1975 in Tehran and placed a bid. Unfortunately, after flying six years for Pan American, I was too junior for the assignment. But I did receive a leave of absence. On December 27th, Ian departed for Tehran. I flew one last round-trip to San Juan before I joined him.

We planned to meet on December 31st in Beirut, Lebanon. Because Ian was off duty over New Year's, we anticipated celebrating that night with his old friend, Saoud. He had invited us to his chalet at the Cedars Ski Resort near Bsharri in the mountains of northern Lebanon. The afternoon of December 31st, I arrived at Beirut Airport on a flight from New York, and Ian flew in from Tehran. A taxi took us to Saoud's place, an 83-mile distance. Ian remembers the two-hour ride as the most horrendous he ever experienced. I recall being terrified as I watched our driver race on unpaved mountain passes, roads without guard rails, and recklessly pass other vehicles. Miraculously, we had no head-on collision.

When we arrived, the sun had set. Saoud and his wife, Yola, welcomed us, offered tea, and suggested a nap. The party began around 11 p.m. and lasted throughout the night. We both recall walking in snow from house to house, visiting Saoud's friends, enjoying the legendary Lebanese hospitality. Conversations ranged between French, English, and Arabic. Music included a melee of rhythmic Middle Eastern tunes with syncopated beats. I joined the dancers, Ian watched. Food was abundant along with drinks, particularly arak, an aniseed-flavored distilled spirit. At daybreak, Saoud insisted we taste Knafeh, a cake made with shredded phyllo dough, ricotta cheese, and sweet rosewater. Then it was time to return to Beirut. A friend of Saoud's provided a ride to the airport where we boarded a Pan American clipper for Tehran. When the plane took off, we did not know we were leaving Beirut for the last time. Four months later, in April 1975, civil war broke out and we never visited Lebanon again.

Ian with Captain Miller Hayes and Paul Claessen, the flight engineer, all dressed for show.

Back in Tehran, Ian left in the early morning for Jeddah, a two and half to three-hour flight. Planes flew continuously on a 24-hour basis with minimum rest periods for flight crews. On occasion I went to the Grand Bazaar and bought caviar to eat in our room after Ian returned from a late-night flight. The hotel's restaurant provided the set-up: a serving dish with ice, lemon wedges, sour cream, toast, minced onions, and hard-boiled eggs, (yolks and whites chopped separately). Sounds decadent? Ian does not think so. As he looks back at that time, he worked hard and deserved the special treat.

Ian had little free time, though one afternoon we visited Iran's Central Bank and admired the Iranian Crown Jewels. The collection is so valuable the jewels are used to back Iran's currency even today. We also took a day trip to Persepolis, Iran's original capital, which dates to 515 B.C. Three years earlier in 1971, the site had been in the news. Shah Reza Pahlavi had invited dignitaries from around the world to attend a lavish party in Persepolis to commemorate the 2500 anniversary of the Persian Empire.

Now, in 1974, Iran Air gave us a free pass for the one and a half-hour flight to Shiraz, an hour's drive from the historic site. Though mostly in ruins, it spreads across a 30-acre raised and walled terrace. Once, as one of the largest cities in Persia, it housed ceremonial halls, palaces, grand gates, staircases, enormous columns, and walls inscribed with bas-relief of animals, lotus flowers, and people.

Ian in Persepolis by wall showing bas-relief of soldiers.

Not wanting to waste an opportunity for another adventure, I felt compelled to observe the hajj operation. I borrowed a uniform and boarded the plane as part of the crew. Flights departed from a special terminal. Pilgrims from all parts of Iran, mostly poor peasants, had never been on a plane. They carried small bundles of belongings, which often included a treasured knife. To their horror, airport personnel confiscated the knives, said they would get them back when they returned to Tehran. Ground agents used sticks to herd people up the stairs to the B-747, which had been configured to hold 500 or more passengers. Every seat on the flight was taken, including upstairs. I occupied a jump seat for take-off. As the aircraft rolled down the runway, people prayed so loudly they drowned out the engines. While I helped serve boxed lunches, I noticed a man had spread and lit a small amount of kindling in the aisle. Pushing the man back into his seat, I yelled, "Fire." In an instant a colleague appeared with an extinguisher. Apparently, the man wanted to heat water for tea. I still wonder what he planned to heat the tea in! Yet, for the most part, the Iranians were pleasant people, humble and grateful for our service. That was a flight to remember!

Our return to New York on January 15th, was equally memorable. Imagine Ian and me with some thirty crewmembers in a vacant B-747, its main galley stocked with food and drinks, plus wine and champagne. The party began not long after take-off from Tehran and lasted six hours until the plane landed in Shannon, Ireland, for refueling and an overnight crew rest for the pilots. That evening, after dinner at the airport hotel, all of us gathered at the bar. A senior male steward played tunes on an old upright piano, while we sang and danced. At the time the merrymaking sounded like a good idea. It did not seem so the following day. Hungover, Ian and I stretched out to sleep in the middle rows of the plane, all the way to New York.

20

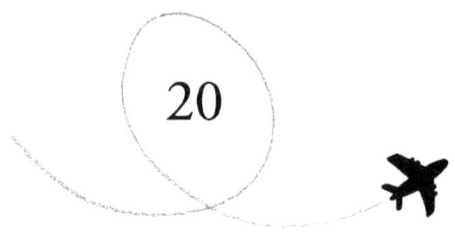

Over dinner in Bayshore, one evening in early 1975, Ian announced that I should have a child. We had not discussed children of our own. His words startled me. I asked what suddenly prompted his desire. He said it was unfair for me to be only a stepmother, that I deserved a child of my own. I wondered if Ian was ready for a new baby. David was a senior in high school, Jim in his sophomore year. Since Ian's divorce, the boys visited regularly during holidays and vacations. In summer, they splashed in our Bayshore pool, went fishing and clamming in the nearby Great South Bay. We sent David to a golf camp. Twice, Jimmy attended a German glider school near Fulda, east of Frankfurt. The brothers had flown to Beirut, spent time with Saoud's family. And Scott, the youngest, traveled with us to Paris and Rome.

At thirty, I knew we should not wait and discontinued the pill. I was pregnant within a few months and stopped working. At the first sign of pregnancy, stewardesses had to inform Pan American or risk losing her job. I was in my fourth month when Ian and I vacationed in the Cayman Islands. On day one, after snorkeling around the reefs, I developed cramping and spotting. Ian took me to a make-shift clinic located in old military barracks. A physician ordered bed rest. My condition did not improve. We flew to Florida. Suffering a miscarriage, I wondered if I was meant to bear a child.

Soon thereafter I returned to work. Meanwhile, Ian was awarded a two-month temporary assignment in Sydney, Australia, that would begin in January of 1976. To join him, I applied for a leave of absence, which was granted. During reduced winter schedules, Pan American was pleased to have stewardesses off the payroll. But on my last trip home that December, I received an in-flight message. The first seven days of my leave had been cancelled. A moment of self-pity turned to anger. Pan American was ruining our plans, and I was not going to allow it. After landing in New York, I went to my supervisor. I reminded her that Pan American had granted me a leave of absence for January and February, which I intended to take. She had two choices, I said. If she could not reinstate the first seven days, I would be sick and remain on Pan American's payroll. On leave, I would be without pay. She granted my request. When Ian heard about it, he admired my chutzpah.

On January 1st, 1976, Ian and I travelled first-class to Australia. We stopped overnight in Honolulu to visit friends and arrived in Sydney the morning of January 4th after crossing the International Date Line. A Pan American agent handed us the keys to a car and a map to Noah's Northside Gardens, an apartment complex in North Sydney. We were exhausted, not used to driving on the left. Somehow, we found the place. If there was an argument about directions (and I am certain there was) it has long since been forgotten. Noah's Northside was a tall building

Ian and Ilona in Sydney, 1976.

in a residential neighborhood. We were shown to a two-bedroom apartment with a spacious living room and a galley kitchen on an upper floor. A small balcony overlooked a sports field. Ian said the balcony was the perfect place for a hibachi grill.

During the next two months, Ian logged thirteen flights, four to five hours each way, to either Nandi on the island of Fiji or Pago-Pago in American Samoa. Because of Pan American's infrequent schedule to the islands, the crews had three to four-day layovers, a perfect timeline to accompany Ian. Pan American gave me free passes. In 1976, few people travelled to the islands, and the planes were never fully booked. Unlike Ian's schedule in Tehran the year before when he flew almost daily, blocks of free time in Sydney allowed us to tour the backcountry of New

South Wales, to lounge on Sydney's beaches, and to vacation in New Zealand. Sadly, a typhoon caused the cancellation of an outing to the Great Barrier Reef. Yet we enjoyed two months of paid vacation.

Soon after returning to New York, I knew I was pregnant, with the baby due on December 25th. I did not fly the rest of the year. Ian, who wanted to attend our child's birth, flew his last trip mid-December. Christmas Day came. No baby. As the year's end approached, Ian worried about his 1976 child tax deduction, suggested I run around the block, jump into a snowbank, do anything to precipitate labor. That Christmas, snow piled around our Bayshore home. It was so cold the Great South Bay froze over. On January first, still no baby. Ian called Pan American scheduling daily, to postpone his flights. At long

Ian, his mother, and Ilons at Alec's baptism.

last, on January 11th, 1977, Alec Douglas came into the world. Ian was present at the birth of our first child. But as soon as I came home from the hospital, he left for Rio. In March 1977, we traveled with Alec to Butler. Wearing an heirloom Duncan christening gown, Alec was baptized in the church his grandparents had joined in 1930.

In November 1977, we bought a house on the western part of Candlewood Lake and moved to New Milford, Connecticut. Nature trails and woods surrounded the property. We thought New Milford, a typical small New England town, was going to be the place we lived until old age. Century-old residences lined both sides of Main Street and the Town-Green. Restored and painted in historic Jewett White, these homes had become offices for banks and law firms. The railroad station was no longer in use, and the depot served as a haunted house at Halloween. It took only minutes to get from the post office to the grocer and the hardware store. A movie theater provided entertainment.

After moving into our new home, Ian's first project was to finish the basement. Though the previous owner had installed a brick fireplace and a bar, its walls were bare cement. Why not panel them with trees from our property? A local lumber mill cut the trees into wide boards, which we dried and planed ourselves, before nailing them to the walls. The agonizing job took over a year.

Ian liked country life. He bought a tractor, became a gardener, and ploughed a small field for tomatoes, zucchini, carrots, onions, Brussel sprouts, and peppers. I asked for a flower bed with zinnias, pink cosmos, and decorative gourds.

Ian with chainsaw, New Milford, Connecticut.

The latter were extremely fruitful. By fall the vines had climbed trees and gourds dangled from branches like Christmas balls.

As a woodsman, Ian was enamored with his chainsaw and liked to fell trees. One of them took off half the deck in front of our house. On another occasion, a Sunday morning in November, I heard a loud bang, and the power went off. Outside Ian stood, chainsaw in hand, looking sheepishly at a downed tree across an electric powerline. Petrified, he remained in place long enough for me to grab my camera to take a photo.

I called *Connecticut Power and Light*, said a fallen tree on our property had caused a power outage. The sequence of events remained in Ian's memory. He was still holding the saw when the power company's truck appeared. Two men got out. One of them grinned and said, "I see a tree has fallen." Not only had the tree taken out our powerline but the district's distribution box. Ian must have charmed them with his sense of humor. They did not report him, which would have been cause for a fine. They left with $20:00 to buy a case of beer. From then on, whenever I saw Ian with a chainsaw, I moved our cars out of reach and took refuge.

Not long after moving to New Milford, Ian befriended airline pilots who shared his interest in hunting the ducks and geese that flew over Candlewood Lake and along the Housatonic River. Unlike the New Jersey ducks, these were edible. Plucking the birds by hand became too tedious, so the trio of pilots decided to jointly own a duck plucker. This mechanized device has small rubber fingers that rotate and pluck feathers. Ian volunteered to house the machine in our basement workshop. Common sense would have installed the plucker inside a container to hold the feathers. Instead, these brainless men placed it on the workbench and held the ducks and geese against it. Feathers everywhere. Long after hunting season was over, I discovered *down* in nooks and corners. That's when I told Ian the plucker had to go. One of Ian's friends offered to house it in his garage. I don't think they used it again.

    Our daughter, Natasha, was born October 1979, and Ian's son Scott had come to live with us. By then, David was a senior at the Air Force Academy, and Jim a student at Embry Riddle University in Daytona, Florida. Then in 1980, Ian's career took a different turn, which caused him to spend less time at home and to forgo most of his hobbies.

21

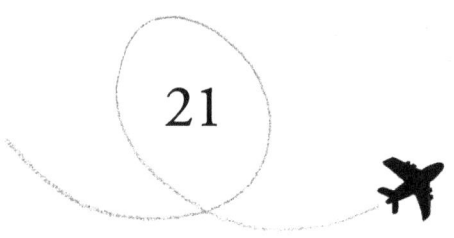

In early 1978, Ian's seniority meant he qualified to become a captain on the Boeing 707. For seven years he had flown copilot on this aircraft. Pan American, nonetheless, required a three-week training in San Francisco. Then in May, in an empty plane over Dulles airport in Virginia, Ian performed all required maneuvers and passed his check ride. A months later on June 24th, Captain Bob Ingalls, a check airman, gave Ian his line check on a military charter from Frankfurt to McGuire AFB in New Jersey. Ian's flawless performance impressed Bob. He recommended that Ian become a check airman at once.

Ian returned home euphoric, eager to share his good news. As a check airman, he would be paid ten percent more than a regular captain, have more flexibility in scheduling, and qualify new captains and copilots. On August 5th, 1978, on a flight from New York to Vienna, Ian's new position became official. Within his seniority group, Ian was unique: the only B-707 captain who became a check airman straight away. The difference on his uniform was hardly noticeable: a wreath around the star above his wings to indicate his new status.

Ian's Pan Am wings.

I asked Ian to explain a check airman's responsibilities. First and foremost, the position required courtesy and respect, he told me. A check airman should compliment success and treat failure with diplomacy. The pilot who made an error did not need to feel crushed. Failing someone was particularly hard when everything had gone well in-flight, but the pilot botched an approach. There were occasions, less than twenty in his career, when Ian gave a pre-warning in case the pilot wanted union representation during debriefing. Ian kept precise records. A failure usually ended in a grievance, which meant Ian had to testify. Problems arose during upgrades to first officer or captain. Some longtime flight engineers needed more time to check out as first officers. Pan American had a specific policy on failures. If a pilot did not pass after several attempts, he had two choices: retire or revert to his old position. Ian ultimately devised a program for additional simulator training. Although costly for Pan American, who paid accommodation, meals, and simulator hours to a non-working pilot, the program was a success. As a result, less than one percent of flight engineers failed to become first officers.

Besides evaluating crewmembers, Ian worked on crew coordination, human factors, and communication. He attended meetings to discuss changes on national or international flight rules. He specifically recalled a new requirement in the early 1980s regarding speed limits. Below ten thousand feet, an aircraft should not exceed 250 knots. In Europe this was strictly mandated. To avoid a fine, a pilot had to slow down at the specific points marked on approach charts.

Captain Duncan and Ilona at the forward door of a B-707 in 1978.

That year in 1978, Ian and I went to his 25th high school reunion in Butler. I met some of his school friends, and Ian introduced me to Joanne who attended with her husband. I remember her as a pleasant woman. During that stay we also visited Phillips Hall. Years before, in the early 1970s, the estate had been for sale. At the time, the Butler Board of Recreation hoped for the state to purchase the property. The *Butler Eagle* reported that the Arts Council intended to use the mansion as an arts center with galleries, workshops, a library, a theater, and the Phillips' pool as a recreation facility. When this did not happen, the property was sold to Ernie Pandelos, an Ohio restaurateur, who converted the Duncan's apartment above the carriage house into a nightclub and the mansion into an upscale restaurant. That summer of 1978, Ian offered to take Isabella and me to lunch there.

She gussied up for the outing. And the following Sunday, Ian guided his mother to a table in the dining room once owned by Mr. Phillips. She wore a suit, hat, gloves, and held a purse on her arm like Queen Elizabeth. Walking behind them, I admired the wood-paneled walls, crystal chandeliers, and tables covered with white linen. Isabella began talking as soon

Phillips Hall, today – The Mansion – *an elegant venue for weddings.*

as our waitress arrived. She said she had lived on the estate and her late husband had worked for Mr. Phillips. "Who was Mr. Phillips?" the young woman asked. As Isabella began to tell the history of Phillips Hall, Ian rolled his eyes. Yet it pleased him the subject was other than his career as a Pan American pilot. Later that day, Ian told me how strange it had felt walking into the mansion he was not allowed to enter in childhood. He had wished, however, that Mr. Phillips were still alive, so he could be updated on Ian's success.

While in Butler, Ian and I spent an afternoon with Mr. Scholter. At sixty-eight, he was retired from Scholter Aviation and lived with his wife in a cottage near the airport. I was delighted to meet the charming man who had encouraged Ian in his youth. While I listened to Ian and Mr. Scholter reminisce, I could sense their mutual friendship and bond. A Boeing 707 model was Ian's gift to the man who had been instrumental in his life.

From 1979 onward, Ian's career escalated. In early 1980, he trained with a Lockheed instructor pilot to become a captain on the L-1011. Flight training was done at Dade-Collier Training and Transition Airport in Florida's Everglades, 36 miles west of Miami. Begun in 1968, the airport was designed to be the largest in the world (five times the size of JFK) and to accommodate supersonic air travel on six runways. At the time, Boeing was developing its B-2707, a supersonic aircraft, larger and faster than Europe's *Concorde*. But rising costs and a questionable market cancelled the program. Subsequently, after the completion of one 10,500-foot runway in 1970, the

Lockheed L-1011.

airport's construction stopped. Dade-Collier became an airfield for general aviation and training.

On May 16th, 1980, on a flight from Miami to Caracas, Ian became a Lockheed L-1011 captain and check airman for that aircraft.

That summer, John Harris, the New York base chief pilot, asked Ian if he could work part time in the chief pilot's office. Ian had flown with John, respected him as a gentleman and pilot, and accepted the request. Before year's end, Ian was appointed Manager-Flying. He became responsible for eight-hundred JFK based pilots and flight engineers, to ensure their competency and qualifications on all Pan American aircraft. In a letter December 3rd, 1980, Captain Harris requested that Ian no longer be a line pilot. (A pilot who is awarded a monthly bidline.)

As manager-flying and later system chief pilot, Ian represented Pan American on the national Air Transport Association (ATA) committee and the International Air Transport Association (IATA). The latter met twice a year, ATA each quarter, to discuss ways to improve flight operations and airport problems. At the time, taxiway lights were a concern. Ian recalled landing at night with good visibility on well-marked runways. But he was in the dark as soon as he turned onto a taxiway. European airports were the first to install taxiway lights. Like street traffic lights, they turned green, amber, and red. Today this is standard in all major airports.

Not long after Ian began work in the chief pilot's office, "flying a desk" as he called it, his pilot seniority allowed him to become captain on the Boeing 747. As he had previously done on the B-707 and L-1011, he completed a pre-command check

Captain Duncan in a B-747 cockpit.

in an empty plane, which included the usual engine failure during take-off, plus an emergency descent. Ian said it was impressive to watch a B-747 nosedive from 37,000 to 14,000 feet, all power pulled back, speed brakes on, with the landing gear down below 20,000 feet. In New York, this pre-command check was done at warning area 106, a specially designed airspace for military aircraft maneuvers over Narraganset Bay. After 1983, Pan American considered the check in the plane too risky and gave only simulator qualifications.

As a management pilot and check airman, Ian was qualified to ferry aircraft with an inoperative engine. We both have distinct memories of an incident on August 10th, 1981. That day, the Paris station manager called the JFK chief pilot's office and told Ian that an L-1011 was stranded at Orly airport. A faulty engine needed replacing, but the nearest location for a new one was London Heathrow. Ian left his office, boarded that evening's New York to Paris flight, and hoped to sleep on the plane.

I happened to be in Paris that night and was scheduled to return to New York the morning of Ian's arrival. Imagine my surprise when I ran into him at Orly Flight Operations. Ian was in a business suit, not in uniform. I asked, "What are you doing here?" He told me he had just arrived from New York, had been unable to go home to change, and was headed to London on a two-engine ferry flight. I noticed how tired he looked. Was he nuts? Would he be able to make the right decisions after having been awake for nearly twenty hours? Ian told me not to worry, that he had agreed to do it because his copilot, who was part of the Paris crew, was also a check airman and trained on two-engine ferries. But he added with a grin that the flight might be tricky if a second engine failed. I was not amused. "Watch me take-off," were his last words before he kissed me goodbye.

That morning, I did not understand why Pan American Flight Operations, aware of the L-1011's engine problem, had directed the cabin crew to leave the downtown Paris hotel and report to Orly. We were to wait for another plane due later that day and spend crew rest at the Orly Hilton. From the window of my hotel room, I had a full view of the airport and watched the L-1011 speed down the runway. It did not climb fast but eventually disappeared into the clouds. I did not know until later, at crew check-in, that Ian had landed safely in London.

We were both back in Connecticut before I learned the details about the flight. Ian said the plane's slow ascent caused the control tower to ask if there was a problem. Ian had not told the tower about the inoperative engine. Because of the proximity to populated areas, Orly had an unwritten rule that no defective plane could be ferried out. There was obviously a reason for this, and I remember voicing my displeasure to Ian about his fearless nature.

"Think of all the money I saved Pan American!" Ian said. He asked if I had any idea of the expense to ship a new engine across the Channel from London to Orly. I did not. A year later, Ian accepted what I considered another risky assignment. To my consternation, it was out of the ordinary flights that thrilled him.

I have a clear recollection of that weekend in August 1982. By then I had retired and was a fulltime mother. Ian was home in Connecticut when a call came from Pan American's director of operational control. I overheard Ian's part of the conversation, as he repeated "classified mission, freighter JFK to Mogadishu, class-A munitions." He then said, "Sure, I'll do it, if you get a volunteer first officer and flight engineer."

"What was that about?" I asked.

"They want me to fly a B-747 freighter with armored vehicles and missiles to Mogadishu."

"Somalia? Are you out of your mind?" I asked if he hadn't done enough military missions in his life. Yet Ian was determined to take the assignment. I reminded him that he had a wife and five children, two under the age of six.

Ian recalled that it was not easy to find volunteers to join him. Still, within twenty-four hours, Gene Turner agreed to be the flight engineer, and Jack Meyers the first officer. Ian did not recall the details of their departure from JFK. His logbook shows he left on Tuesday evening, August 24th, and arrived the following morning at Ramstein Air Force Base, Germany. After a twenty-four-hour rest period, the crew would continue to Mogadishu after a refueling stop in Cairo.

On the day of their departure from Ramstein, the three men wondered about the routing. The cargo's explosive nature prohibited flights over Austrian, Italian, and Swiss airspace. France was the only option to reach the Mediterranean and circumvent Italy. Prior to departure, an Air Force intelligence

235

officer said the crew would be required to fly 'radio silent' from Cairo southward. This was news to Ian. Still, the trio agreed to continue the mission. The plane, heavily loaded with rifles, fifty-caliber ammunition, rocket-propelled grenades, and armored personnel carriers, took off that evening for the four-hour flight to Cairo. After refueling, the crew continued south to Somalia. Ian recalled the eerie silence as they flew in darkness over the Red Sea. The only contact during the 5 ½ hour flight was an hourly call via Bern radio in Switzerland to Pan American Dispatch. Once the plane reached the Horn of Africa, there was fear that Ethiopia and Yemen might launch ground to air missiles. Flight Engineer Gene said there was enough fuel to raise the power to Mach .88, which would cut the transit time by ten minutes. Ian recalled numerous warnings over the radio. "Aircraft heading at high-speed NW of Addis Ababa identify yourself." The crew ignored the warnings. The AF intelligence officer had told them Ethiopia had no aircraft capable of intercepting the 747. Yet Ian and his fellow crewmen were relieved to reach the Indian Ocean and make their first radio call to Mogadishu. The plane landed in early morning and was quickly unloaded. After a crew rest, they began an eight-hour flight to Frankfurt.

    At home, I anxiously awaited word of Ian's safe return. Without cellphones we could not communicate, and oversea calls on landlines were terribly expensive. Relief came when crew scheduling informed me that Ian was back in Frankfurt and would be on a flight home on August 30th.

After Ian became manager-flying late in 1980, he was seldom home. When not piloting a plane, he worked in his JFK office. His daily commute, in traffic 2 ½ hours each way from New Milford to JFK, took its toll. He rarely arrived home before 9:00 p.m. and left again by 6:00 in the morning. Wintry weather made the drive treacherous. We both agreed the daily routine was detrimental to his health. Plus, Ian rarely saw his children. Jim was bitterly disappointed in 1982 when his father did not attend his college graduation. In spring 1983, Ian finally resolved to resign as manager-flying and return to flying captain on the B-747. His schedules took him back to Europe, South America, and Asia. Most flights had been routine. Yet Ian remembered a certain departure to Rome in the summer of 1983.

Thunderstorms had formed late that afternoon near JFK as the heavy B-747, with a full load of passengers, left the gate. Ian's plane joined others 'in elephant walk', one aircraft lined behind the others. When Ian reached the take-off position, his cockpit radar showed a massive airmass two miles ahead. Large downbursts were advancing toward the end of the runway. He told the controller that he preferred not to take off and asked where he should wait out the storm. He was told to taxi and sit. The captain in the plane behind Ian thought that was a good idea and requested the same. So did the one behind him, and every plane thereafter received a parking position. For thirty minutes, they waited. A longer period would have necessitated refueling. Eventually, Ian took off. Point of the story? If Ian hadn't said he preferred not to take off, would the other ten planes behind him have gone? Pilots can manifest a bravado. If he can, I can, too. Ian said it was a hard pattern for male pilots

to break. That day, his caution and prudence may have averted a catastrophe.

Another flight of note was later that year on November 8th, 1983, to accompany President Reagan to Japan and Korea. In the early 1980s, Ian flew several White House press charters. Only four captains, eight copilots, and six flight engineers had been cleared by the presidential security office to fly the press corps, which included camera men, photographers, journalists, and television crews, usually over two-hundred persons. The day Ian flew the press to Japan, security was on high alert. Two months earlier, on September 1st, 1983, a Korean B-747 had veered slightly off course and been shot down. The Russians had spotted the plane on radar and thought it was a U.S. reconnaissance plane spying on Kamchatka peninsula's military installations.

That November 8th, before they took off from Elmendorf AFB near Anchorage, Ian and the captain on Air Force One devised a strategy to confuse the Russians. Air Force One normally left first. The plane with the press then passed it, in order to be on the ground for the president's arrival. This time both captains opted to fly side by side at the same speed until they reached Alaska's west coast. Only then did Ian's plane take the lead. Communications were over a special frequency with minimum talk until Haneda Airport near Tokyo. If the Russians had any inclination to sabotage the president's plane,

The crew received cufflinks with the presidential seal.

they would not have known which one was Air Force One. Both captains repeated the maneuvers on their way to Seoul and back to Elmendorf.

In early 1984, one year after resigning from his position as manager-flying, Ian invited Captain Don Pritchett, Pan American's V.P. Flight Operations, for a weekend in our New Milford home. Recently separated from his wife, Don came alone. On Sunday morning after breakfast, he took me aside, and said he wanted to discuss a matter in private. The word 'private' gave me an uneasy feeling. Why the secrecy? What could be so important? I don't remember where Ian was at that moment. He might have gone upstairs to the bedroom. I sat down with Don at the kitchen table. Then, with some hesitancy, he asked for my permission to have Ian resume working at JFK. Don hoped Ian would take the position as Pan American's system chief pilot. I asked why he sought my permission, said Ian could make his own choices, that I would never impede or influence my husband's career.

In the spring of 1984, Ian became system chief pilot in charge of all Pan American crew bases: New York, Los Angeles, San Francisco, Seattle, Miami, and Berlin, in Germany.

22

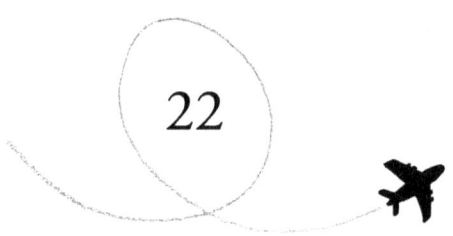

As system chief pilot, Ian operated minimum flights on the L-1011 and the B-747, enough to stay current (three take-offs and landings within three months). In August 1984, he flew a B-707 one last time, from New York to Houston. The flight was non-commercial, which meant that Ian did not need to be current. The aircraft, the last of Pan American's B-707 fleet, had been sold to a company that marketed buffalo meat. I asked, "You mean they loaded buffalos into a 707?" Ian grinned and said, "Not allowed in first. Had to travel cattle class." A befitting answer to a silly question, and Ian did not know what became of the aircraft.

The same year, 1984, Airbus Industrie, the European airplane manufacturer, made a deal to sell sixteen A-300 aircraft to Pan American. The sale was a breakthrough for Airbus. Until then, the European manufacturer had been unsuccessful in persuading U.S. airlines to buy its planes. In appreciation, Airbus rented New York's Museum of Modern Art and invited Pan American officials, including Ian and me, to a catered black-tie dinner. The Glenn Miller orchestra provided the music. I recall dancing late into the night. It would be the first of many memorable Airbus events we attended.

Pan American spent over a billion for the Airbus planes, with an option of forty more in the future. This was an enormous amount for an airline that had lost 650 million in the past three years. In 1981 to generate funds, Pan American had sold its Intercontinental Hotel division and the Pan Am building in Manhattan. The cash-strapped airline blamed its problem on subsidized competition and asked its workforce

Pan Am Base News cartoon, 1981.

243

for concessions. From that period, Ian kept a JFK Flight Operations news bulletin. A cartoon in it caught my attention.

A year later on April 23rd, 1985, major newspapers announced Pan American's sale of its Pacific routes to United Airlines. Before it became world news, Ian called me at home. He said pilots would be part of the deal. I asked, "You are going to work for United?" Ian said he could, but his seniority would make him a junior captain in Los Angeles. This meant for the first year or more, he would be on standby without a fixed schedule. Given that Pan American's financial troubles worried me, I thought Ian should consider this. But he had made up his mind not to live in Los Angeles.

Regardless of the company's economic situation, Pan American acquired seven A-310 aircraft in 1986. This plane's two Pratt & Whitney 4000 engines were more economical to operate, which meant two A-310s used less fuel to cross the Atlantic than one B-747. Airbus commemorated the successful sale with a Christmas gala at Windows of the World, a restaurant on the 107th floor of the World Trade Center. Ian and I joined Pan American's managing staff and wives for the lavish gala. We could not have predicted that within two years Ian would be part of the Airbus team.

Ian did not fly the A-300 or the A-310. Yet as system chief pilot, he oversaw the initial training, the check airmen selection, route proofing, and FAA approval. He made several trips to Toulouse, France, and met with the Airbus flight training

System Chief Pilot Duncan in his JFK office with an A-310 model.

department, which at the time was co-owned by Flight Safety International, a U.S. company with aircraft training centers around the United States and Canada. The meetings would open new flight plans in Ian's future.

One of Ian's more memorable events as system chief pilot involved the hijacking of Pan American flight 73 on September 5th, 1986. He was on his way home to Connecticut at the time the assault occurred. When his pager went off, he called Operations Control and learned a B-747 from Bombay

(Mumbai) to New York had been hijacked during a stopover in Karachi.

Since the late 1960s, commercial aviation had become a target for terrorism. It seemed easy for a few persons to seize and take control of an aircraft. In 1970, a Pan American B-747 was blown up in Cairo after the hijackers released passengers and crew. Terrorists in 1973 stormed up the stairs of a B-747 during a stopover in Rome, threw hand grenades, and killed 34 people including the captain's wife in first class. In August 1982, a bomb went off on a flight from Tokyo to Honolulu, killing one passenger and wounding fourteen. The captain of the flight was able to land safely.

That Friday evening in September, Ian hurried back to his office at Hangar-14, considering scenarios. What were the hijackers' demands? Would they destroy the plane and kill people? A red binder in Ian's office had emergency instructions and checklists for every crisis: crashes, runway excursions, and hijacking. Ian grabbed the binder and raced the short distance to Pan American's command post. The room filled quickly. At a long table, the heads of maintenance, marketing, public relations, dispatch, and finance took seats. A phone was at each place. Ian represented Flight Operations and arranged for an airplane to fly Pan American's chairman, Mr. Edward Acker, back to New York from the ATA conference in Casper, Wyoming.

Then Ian heard details of the hijacking via a hotline with Karachi Flight Operations. At 4:30 a.m. local time (7:30 p.m. the day before in New York), four heavily armed men, dressed as airport security guards, had arrived by van, and fired shots as they ran up the stairs to the B-747. It was later determined the four were Palestinians of the Abu Nidal Organization (ANO). One of the flight attendants alerted the cockpit. The three pilots evacuated through an overhead escape hatch via inertial reels alongside the fuselage. Once on the ground, they ran to Pan American Operations. When Ian learned this, he ordered them to take a taxi, not the usual limo, and head to the U.S. embassy. Next, he alerted the State Department. By then, a Delta Force C-130 had taken off from an airbase in the Middle East, been directed to hold over Karachi, and await the command to storm the B-747. Meanwhile, Pakistani military had surrounded the airport.

At some point Ian called me to say he was not coming home that night. Then, craving a cigarette, he borrowed coins to buy a pack from a vending machine near Pan American's cafeteria. His efforts to quit smoking had lasted two weeks.

On the hijacked B-747 were 365 passengers and 16 flight attendants, Indian nationals based in New Delhi. The terrorists' plan was to fly to Israel, then Cyprus, and demand that both nations release ANO prisoners. One of the hijackers used the radio on the engineer's panel to make their demand for pilots. ANO's threat was to kill a passenger every ten minutes until a new cockpit crew was in place. To make their point, one of the terrorists shot a Navy man in uniform and threw his body from an open exit door.

Ian, hoping to locate an Arabic speaking crew, tried to get in touch with Saoud, his longtime Lebanese friend. When Saoud was unreachable, Ian called IATA contacts. The Middle

East Airlines (MEA) V.P. Flight Operations, a B-747 captain, volunteered to fly to Karachi with a new crew. But MEA's chairman did not approve because he thought this action would be detrimental to both the airline and Beirut Airport. Hours went by. Ian remembered numerous phone calls and trying to locate a cockpit crew. At long last, Hart Langer, a friend and management pilot who happened to be on a Hamburg layover, agreed to take the hijackers wherever they wanted to go as long as they let the passengers off. First Officer Ed Cywinski and Flight Engineer Bob Huettl joined Hart. The three headed on a commercial flight to Karachi.

By early morning on September 6th in New York, Ray Valeika, the V.P. of Pan American's maintenance department, predicted the plane's auxiliary power unit (APU) would shut down. This electrical unit burned high amounts of oil and would fail under low oil pressure. Meanwhile in Karachi, it was nightfall, and the plane sat in darkness. Fifteen hours into the hijacking, the terrorists were increasingly impatient and agitated. Then, as predicted, at 9:30 p.m., the APU failed. The cabin lights went off. Panic and bedlam. The hijackers tried to throw hand grenades but did not fully pull the pins. This caused only small explosions. A flight attendant yelled to open all door and window exits. Passengers scrambled to escape despite the gunfire. But the exit slides, disarmed during the stopover, could not be deployed. This forced the passengers to jump fifteen feet from the aircraft or run out over the wings. The defeated terrorists tried to flee, but the Pakistani military captured them.

Seventeen hours into the hijacking, the ordeal ended.

At the command post, Ian had been without sleep for close to thirty hours and stayed awake on coffee. He called to say he would be home later that evening. In view of the hours that Ian had been without sleep, I urged him to spend the night at JFK. I should have known he would not listen.

In Karachi, Hart Langer and his crew landed. Three London-based mechanics were summoned to make temporary repairs on the damaged B-747. The plane had 57 bullet holes, which needed to be sealed before Hart and his crew could take off for New York. It took five days before the aircraft was certified to fly. But Boeing restricted it to partial pressurization, which meant flying below 25,000 feet. This required additional fuel, and a stopover for crew rest in Frankfurt.

When the plane landed at JFK, Ian was waiting. He thanked the crew for their efforts. Then he inspected the plane's interior with its torn fabric, dried blood, and putrid odor. He would not get more graphic than that, he said. Pan American's insurance covered the cost for repair, and the aircraft was put back in service under a new name: *Clipper New Horizons*. (The previous name was *Clipper Empress of the Seas*.) Because the hijacking was an act of aggression, State Department paid for personal injuries. Twenty-one people were killed, 120 injured. Neerjah Bhanot, a beautiful and courageous Indian stewardess, lost her life while shielding children from bullets.

The hijackers were tried in a Pakistani court and sentenced to death. The verdict was later converted to a life sentence. In

2008, Pakistan deported the prisoners to Palestine. They remain on the FBI's most wanted list. Libya, accused of sponsoring the attack, denied involvement. Five years later, Pan American flight 103 exploded over Lockerbie, Scotland.

A week after the horrific event, Ian was grateful for a long weekend with airline managers at a fishing camp near North Bay, some 200 miles north of Toronto. The host, Harvey Watt, formerly with Eastern Airlines, insured pilots against loss of license. As a payback, he rented the camp's facility year after year during September; and on a rotation, he invited airline managers and executives. This was Ian's sixth trip to the camp, a ritual that began in 1981 when he was manager-flying. I was not pleased to see him go. As it was, I thought he spent too little

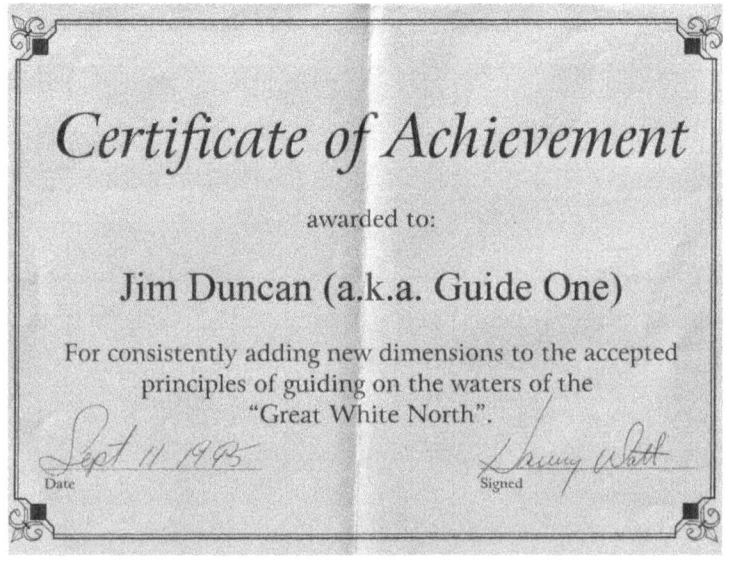

time at home. But Ian argued that the weekend was a chance to trade ideas with other airline managers. I knew better. Ian and his buddies from United, Continental, and Delta, spent all day fishing for walleye and then played poker at night. Once, Ian was lucky and returned with three hundred dollars. Even after Ian got a boat stuck on the lake and was ridiculed as 'Guide One' by his fellow airline buddies, he returned to the camp for another sixteen years. The annual outing meant a lot to Ian. Fishing was not the only attraction. This was a rare occasion to be around males, other than his office staff and pilots, and embrace an informal camaraderie with airline friends.

On Feb 24th, 1987, three years after Ian was appointed system chief pilot, the Pan American board of directors elected him as vice president of Flight Operations. That spring, in an optimistic letter to airmen, Ian tried to boost their morale. Summer bookings were strong, he wrote. Recent concessions with labor associations had raised the company's financial profile and after eighteen years, furloughed pilots had been recalled.

Ian's accomplishments were exceptional. I will admit I loved his new position, which had the advantage of first-class, positive space, travel. But except for weekends, we lived apart. Ian stayed Monday through Friday at the Marriot near JFK, while I lived in New Milford with the children. By then, Scott had enlisted in the Air Force and been assigned to Germany. Rural life had lost its appeal. I felt alone and frustrated. Even on family vacations, Ian was called back to work, which left me alone with Alec and Natasha. Repeatedly, after becoming system chief pilot in 1984, Ian had assured me that his position in management was temporary. "I'll go back to line flying and be home more often." In April 1987, my patience ran out. When he returned home late one Friday evening, I said I was going to move. He could come with me or not. Ian knew when I had a plan, I would implement it. Without hesitation, he told me to search for a house close to JFK, so he could be home every night. By August's end we moved to Stamford, Connecticut, and Pan American paid for the relocation.

The year Ian became V.P. Flight Operations, Pan American sponsored *A Day in the Life of the Soviet Union*. This large, glossy book of photography depicted daily life in the country that four years later was called Russia. That 'one day' was May 15th, 1987, when fifty world-leading photographers positioned themselves all over the Soviet Union. At the time this meant some 7,000 miles from Kaliningrad to the Bering Sea, and from Samarkand in southern Uzbekistan to Northern Siberia. The result was a photographic journey, with scenes both positive and negative that few outsiders had seen. Inside the book, on a full page under the blue Pan Am logo, Chairman Acker had a message for the reader; that the book's photographic collection represented a new era of openness and understanding between the Soviet Union and the United States.

The book fascinated Ian. In December 1987, he mailed copies to various friends and acquaintances in the industry. Three letters of acknowledgement have survived: one from Allan McArtor, head of the FAA, another from Russell Meyer,

A Day in the Life of the Soviet Union.

chairman of Cessna aircraft, and the third from Paul Bancroft, the CEO of Bessemer Securities Corporation. The book has been in our library since 1987 and moved with us from Connecticut to France, from Miami to Virginia.

The same year as the book's publication, Pan American acquired Ransome Airlines, renamed it Pan Am Express. This small airline was supposed to serve as a feeder to major hubs. Ian was involved in negotiating a contract between the Air Line Pilot Association (ALPA) and Pan Am Express. His plan was to place all Pan Am Express pilots at the bottom of the current Pan American pilot seniority list. Recently, Pan American had recalled all former furloughed pilots. But a new-hire program had not begun. The agreement was an advantage for former Ransome pilots and provided crossover rights to the parent company. Ian recalls that Ransome's former chief pilot from Philadelphia immediately became a B-737 copilot, and two years later he was a captain. The contract also reduced Pan American's labor costs because the newly hired Pan Am Express pilots were on a lower pay scale.

The magazine, *Air Transport World* (ATW), honored Ian and gave him their annual labor relations award. From 1974 until now, the magazine has given only eight or nine yearly awards from categories that the ATW's editors developed.

Capt. Jim Duncan at the ATW award ceremony with John L. Finley, Managing Director Federal Express.

Selection is based on technology, financial management, industry service, passenger service, technical management, and general excellence among major, world-wide airlines. Ian received his award at a luncheon in the Grand Ballroom of New York's Plaza Hotel.

In February 1988, Gere D. Coffey, publisher of ATW, personally congratulated Ian in a letter and invited him to be a member of the award's jury. He also asked Ian to attend the following year's award ceremony. Little did Ian know that by then, we would be living in Toulouse, France.

23

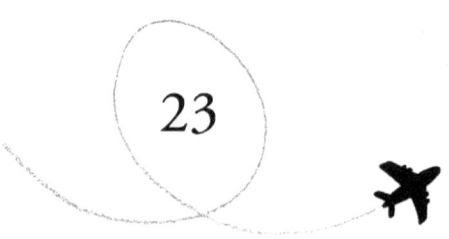

As V.P. Flight Operations in 1987, Ian strove to maintain a trusting relationship with Pan American pilots. His challenge was to negotiate peaceful solutions between management and the union. Meanwhile behind the scenes, Chairman Acker plotted for a deal with Jay Pritzker, the owner of Braniff Airways. Acker believed a merger with Braniff was Pan American's only hope for survival. The deal required 200 million dollars in union concessions, mainly from pilots. Pan American's vice chairman, Marty Shugrue, opposed it. At a December 1987 boardroom meeting, Shugrue and Acker were so enraged they got into a brawl. The directors were incensed. A month later at the January board meeting, after squeezing 180 million in concessions from the unions, Shugrue announced his own proposal. Discussions about a Braniff merger ceased. The price for the deal? Chairman Acker had to go.

For some time, the board had disapproved of Acker. The directors believed he had wasted the proceeds from the Pacific sale by launching in 1986, the Pan Am Shuttle, a route system between Boston, Washington, and La Guardia, New York. The board would have preferred a strong domestic feeder network to serve Pan American's international hubs. Instead, Acker created the Shuttle, a break-even operation. But the search for a new chairman proved difficult. Who would want to head the already troubled airline? Pan American needed a dynamic, charismatic leader who could unite its workforce and mend the chasm that management had created in recent years. Then, on January 20th, 1988, the board announced Thomas Plaskett as the new chairman. He had begun at American Airlines, then rose to the position of senior V.P. of marketing, and introduced AAdvantage, the first frequent flyer program. In 1986, Plaskett became president of Continental Airlines. But Frank Lorenzo, Continental's CEO, did not like Plaskett's lackluster personality and fired him within a year. The board, nonetheless, considered him the best man to save Pan American.

Plaskett's first agenda in the position was to create a new management team. He fired Russel Thayer, the senior V.P. of Operations, and gave Robert Gould the position. Gould had been hired as a pilot, became a union representative, then manipulated himself into Pan American's management. As soon as he was V.P. of Operations, Gould declared he would take over Ian's office and headquarter himself at both JFK and the former Pan Am building in Manhattan. Ian was not surprised that Gould wanted him gone. As manager-flying, Ian had ordered Gould to rehabilitate himself and take a year off. Gould had been found drunk in his hotel room after failing to appear for a scheduled flight simulator session in Miami. Though Gould was later reinstated without loss of seniority, he held a grudge against Ian. The day he entered Ian's office, Gould said he had nothing personal against Ian but could not work with him. Ian said his office would be vacated by the end of the day. Next, he called me.

"I just quit."

"Quit what? Smoking?"

"I was fired today."

I sat down to digest the news. Ian said he would pack things in his office and be home for dinner. "Be happy. I'll go back to flying captain on the 747 and be home more often." I said I would have a drink ready for him.

That same day Gould named Ian's successor. It was Dan Affourtit, a west-coast line pilot and long-time member of Gould's union (ALPA) clique. The announcement outraged Pan American pilots. They were shocked to see a union hack replace Ian, a highly respected and experienced V.P. of Flight Operations. Ned Brown, the director of the Pan American Training Academy was irate and quit his position the same day, stating he would not work for Gould. Ian arranged to meet Dan, his successor, at the International Hotel at JFK and brief him on impending items. Dan was grateful, had nothing but good words to say to Ian. So did hundreds of employees and pilots. Yet many remained in shock. They liked Ian because he supported them and had emphasized safety and pride in their work. Letters of appreciation arrived. Terry G. wrote that Ian's appointment as V.P. Flight Operations had raised the morale of the pilot group when communications between management and pilots had reached their lowest level. He thanked Ian for restoring trust, remaining accessible to the line pilot and, and showing compassion toward individual airmen. A. Lenzi, the chairman and Pan Am Master Executive Council (MEC) of ALPA expressed the MEC's gratitude for Ian's dedicated service to the airline and its pilots. He thanked Ian for not allowing an 'us' versus 'them' attitude to stand between Flight Operations and line pilots. At the time, it was uncommon for pilots and management to be on friendly terms. Bob Durant, another pilot, sent Ian a note and quoted Hamlet: "So excellent a king, that was; to this, Hyperion to a Satyr." Two years would pass before Ian saw Dan Affourtit at an ATA meeting. Dan greeted Ian warmly and said, "You know, Duncan, you're still known at Pan American Operations as King James."

After leaving his position in Flight Operations, Ian cherished his time at home. He took a month of vacation and focused on his health. He vowed to quit smoking, shed the extra pounds gained from 'flying a desk' and prepared menus from diet magazines. Delighted that Ian was cooking a meal, I encouraged him. Alec, to please his father, helped calculate the calories. Natasha wondered why the sudden overabundance of salads and vegetables on the dinner menu. Ian lost weight, quit smoking, and looked fit before he returned to flying. On Saint Patrick's Day, 1988, Ian was back in the cockpit, flying from New York to Los Angeles.

Meanwhile, in the airline industry word got around that Ian had left management. The president of ATW shared Ian's phone number with companies that showed an interest in hiring him. Ian responded to inquiries but made it clear that he would not work for Flight Operations. He said to deal with senior management, the union, pilots, and complainers all at once, was to fall into a briar patch. No matter how attractive the compensation, he promised himself and me to avoid this assignment.

Sometime in April, Al Ueltschi called. He was the president and founder of Flight Safety International and offered Ian a position. Ian said he would think about it but conveyed that he was happy flying the B-747. Days later, Bruce Whitman, Flight Safety's vice president, suggested a meeting at their La Guardia office. Ian went but returned unenthusiastic. The company was vague about his official title, and Ian would only accept a top position. One evening, shortly thereafter, Ian spoke for an unusually long time on the phone. After he hung up, I asked who it was.

"Jean Pinet. He wants me to work for Airbus and move to Toulouse."

"When can I pack?" France! This sounded too good to be true. I had lived there, loved the country, spoke the language fluently. Ian was quick to subdue my ardent enthusiasm. But he agreed to meet with Jean, who happened to be in Miami. Jean was the director of *Aéroformation*, Airbus training in Toulouse, and had known Ian since 1984, the year Pan American pilots trained on the A-300. In late April, Ian flew to Miami. He returned uncommitted and, to my chagrin, had begun smoking again.

More phone calls came from Flight Safety's Bruce Whitman. Each time, he offered higher compensation and profits: foreign allowance, paid move, benefits for children and family. I asked why Flight Safety was so keen on Ian taking the position in Toulouse. Ian wondered the same. He knew only that, when Airbus began building commercial aircraft in the 1970s, Flight Safety provided the training, and had established the *Aéroformation* learning center at Toulouse-Blagnac. Although Airbus took over most of the training in the 1980s, Flight Safety would have a controlling interest until 1992. Ian did not know then that Flight Safety and Airbus wanted Ian to spend time in Toulouse, to know the Airbus system, then have him replace the head of Airbus training in Miami. Ian was an asset because he knew the training methods and regulations. Plus, he had buddies worldwide in the airline business. Years later, Bruce Whitman admitted that Ian was in line to become his deputy, if the Miami deal did not work out.

That Spring of 1988, Ian vacillated from day to day. He feared leaving Pan American, losing his coveted seniority number, not ever flying again. Was he at fifty-three, ready to embark on a whole new career and live in France without speaking French? What if Alec and Natasha hated life there? Granted, if things did not work out, he could become a captain for Singapore Airlines or Korean Air. Both were hiring B-747 pilots. But that was not how Ian wanted his career to end. I understood his dilemma but felt uneasy about Pan American's dire finances.

Then in early May, we were on our way home from a Broadway performance of *Les Misérables* when Ian said he'd made up his mind. He would resign from Pan American the following day and accept the Airbus offer. I wondered what it was about the musical that had triggered his decision. I did not ask, though told Ian I was pleased. When Ian reneged on his words the following morning, I went into a rage. "Pan American is sinking like the Titanic. Do you want all of us to go down with it?" Ian picked up the phone, accepted the position, and then told Pan American he would retire the end of June.

That same month, on May 6th, Ian's mother died at 88. Her death was expected. She had been ailing for some time and lived out her remaining years with Ian's sister Helen in New Jersey. The entire Duncan clan gathered on May 21st at Butler's Covenant United Presbyterian church, where Isabella had been a member since 1930. Her final resting place is next to George's at Greenlawn Burial Estate.

Isobel (left), *Ian and Helen in 1988.*

A week later, Ian and I spent three days in Toulouse. Airbus initiated the paperwork for his French work permit and residency status. I surprised M. and Mme Pinet over dinner at *le Jardin de l'Opéra* with my fluency in French. With the help of a broker, I located a three-story downtown house on rue Agathoise. Ian and I signed a rental agreement, bought all necessary appliances, and directed they be installed before our arrival in early July. French rentals do not include a dishwasher, oven, refrigerator, washing machine, and dryer. I also enrolled Alec and Natasha in a nearby French Catholic school for the upcoming year.

On June 20th, I accompanied Ian on his final flight from Rome to New York. He had been with Pan American for 25 years.

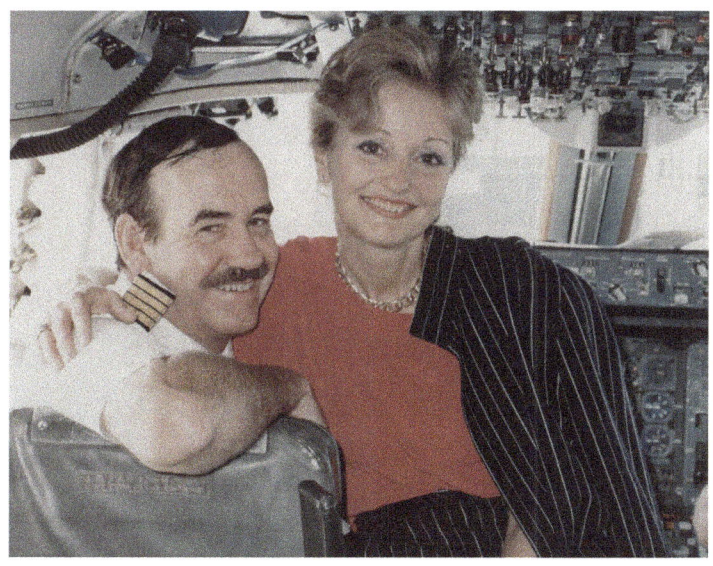

Ian and Ilona in the 747 cockpit in Rome before his final flight.

24

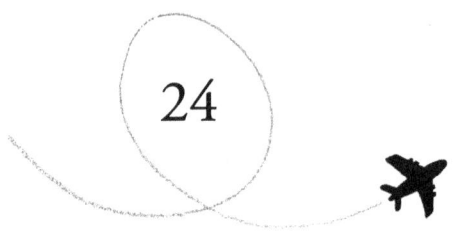

Our departure for France was scheduled for July 7th, 1988, seventeen days after Ian's final flight for Pan American. Flight Safety had booked us on Continental Airlines from New York to Paris, and on Air Inter to Toulouse. I discovered, however, that Continental did not allow a cat in the cabin, though Air France did. For Sonya, our Siamese, to be with us in business class, Ian insisted that Flight Safety change the reservation to Air France.

For days, the movers crated and packed. Our cars had been sold, and Ian ordered a taxi to be at the house no later than 3 p.m. on July 7th. But he was worried the movers would not be finished loading the shipping container by then. He wanted to see the container locked and gone before we left. When this looked impossible, I called our real estate agent. I asked her to come at once, then wait for the movers to leave, and to lock the house.

Ian's sister Helen and her husband met us at the Air France first-class lounge. Ian had urged Helen not to make the 120-mile drive from her New Jersey home. But Helen felt because her brother and family were leaving the country for good, they deserved a formal sendoff. We had a glass of champagne and toasted new beginnings in Toulouse. Miss Sonya was not pleased and yowled until a valium put her to sleep.

We landed at Toulouse-Blagnac Airport the afternoon of July 8th. An Airbus employee met us in the arrival hall and drove Ian to fetch our car, a small Peugeot. I took Alec, Natasha, and whining Sonya in a taxi to our new home. There, a notary awaited us. Her job was to show us around, ascertain that nothing inside was defective, and have the occupancy certificate signed. Once inside the house, Natasha let Sonya out of the carrier. Like a captured creature released into the wild, she tore off to places unknown. Meanwhile, on a tour of the house, I was pleased to see the appliances I'd purchased a month earlier, installed as promised. And because our furniture would not arrive for some time, the homeowner had provided beds and a dining table with four chairs. The boxes shipped by air were in the kitchen and contained essential items: towels, bed sheets, cookware, dishes, cat food, and litter.

Everything at the house seemed in proper working condition until I noticed a broken window on the second floor. Added to this, the door to the courtyard would not lock. The notary placed a call from her portable phone to the owner. Then she told me it might take a day or two for the repairs and in the interim we could not stay there. I felt discombobulated and knew Ian would be irate. But where was he? I looked at my watch. Almost an hour had passed since we parted. No way to reach him. Meanwhile I put food out for Sonya and spread cat litter in the tiled courtyard.

What a relief when Ian walked in. "What happened to you?" I asked. Abashed, Ian said he had been lost and could not understand the French road signs. I chuckled but Ian was not amused. I suggested a practice run the following day. Then I gave the unwelcome news that we couldn't stay. Ian did not seem to understand. I told him some items in the house needed to be repaired and we had to stay in a hotel. "Jesus H. Christ," Ian said, shaking his head in disbelief. He asked the notary to call Airbus and arrange for a hotel. That afternoon we moved into the Hotel De Paris in the center of town. And because July 8th was a Friday, work at the house had to wait until Monday. We remained in the hotel over the weekend but had a key so we could go to the house and feed poor Sonya.

Our new home was a remodeled 250-year-old house with lofty ceilings and french double windows. Each room had an ornately framed fireplace, though none were in working order. Instead, a central heating system with hot water radiators warmed the house in winter. To the right of the entrance hall on the ground floor was a study. Behind it was the living room with french doors that opened to a glass-roofed dining room. A modern kitchen was beside it. A glass wall and door separated the dining room from an interior courtyard and an annex. The chartreuse, as Toulouse residents call this type of dwelling, served as our guest quarters.

 A winding staircase with a wood railing led from the entrance hall to the first floor's master bedroom with its balconette and views of neighboring roofs. Sonya soon discovered this exit. She jumped from the balconette onto the glass-roof above the dining room, then explored adjoining gables, and scared away any bird that settled near chimneys. On the same floor was Natasha's bedroom with Juliet balconies that overlooked the street. Alec's domain was in the *grenier*, the attic beneath an angled roof. Bedrooms had built-in wall-to-wall closets, and each room had its own bathroom, a luxury in old French homes.

That first week, Ian went daily to *Aéroformation*. But he discovered that few persons were at work, in anticipation of Bastille Day, July 14th. Plus, the French were on summer vacation. *France Telecom* and *Électricité de France* ran on reduced personnel, which meant we had to wait two weeks for an increase in the electrical supply to the house. And to Ian's consternation, the wait was even longer for a functioning phone line. Yet an unexpected, pleasant surprise was a neighbor who welcomed us with a stack of crêpes.

By the end of July, the container with our belongings arrived. Police closed *rue Agathoise* for traffic that morning and escorted the truck to our house. Ian made it his job to supervise the unloading. This exacerbated the movers, who spoke only French. "Où?" they asked while pointing to a piece of furniture, hoping to be directed to the right room. "Iloonaaa!" I raced out and told the man to follow me. I wish I knew the number of steps I took that day. The following morning, Ian wisely went to his office while the men unpacked crates and boxes.

The month of August with an oppressive heat felt long. To keep the house cool, I closed the window shutters by 10 a.m. I had bought light fixtures for every room and an electrician installed them. Ian bought a television. For lack of anything to do, Alec and Natasha watched American cartoons dubbed in French, then surprised me with newly learned words. We also had a video recorder, one that played tapes in dual modes: the American NTSC version, and the French PAL. I had bought the device before our departure at a foreign appliance store in Manhattan. Ian's son Jim taped movies and televisions shows in the States and shipped the tapes to us.

Mid-August, I heard about a beachside condo for rent on the Mediterranean coast. Ian remained in Toulouse to work while Alec, Natasha, Sonya, and I joined thousands of beachgoers for a week by the sea. At the beginning of September, I walked Alec and Natasha to school and handed them over to their teachers. Since neither child spoke French, they were held back a year. Some of their classmates went home during the two-hour lunch break. I wanted Alec and Natasha to be with French children and learn to communicate. For this reason, I paid for lunches at school and provided the requested white cloth napkins with sewn-in name tags.

The initial school weeks were difficult. Alec, in fifth grade, required my help. I sat next to him in class and translated each subject. Natasha, in second grade, took to French more easily. She learned basic spelling along with her classmates. But Alec could not follow lessons in math, history, geography, French dictation, and reading. One morning the phone rang. I answered and heard, "This is Yves. Your son is at school with my son. I heard Alec does not speak French. My wife and I would like to help. *"Mais je parle Français,"* I said, and thanked him for the kind offer. I said I would teach Alec but appreciated help. Yves passed the phone to his wife. Ever since that telephone call, Dany and Yves have been our friends.

For the remainder of that first schoolyear and until Alec caught up with his classmates, I translated his lessons and taught him French. Natasha ended up the best in her class. When Ian was not present, the three of us spoke French, not English. Both children eventually served as Ian's translator.

Ian adapted easily to the way of life in France, in particular to the cuisine. Like most Europeans, employees at Airbus ate their main meal at lunchtime. The cafeteria served a four-course repast at the cost of twelve francs (two dollars). On occasion, Ian joined co-workers at a local restaurant. French men did not expect another full course meal at dinner and were content with a snack or a bowl of soup. Not Ian. He wanted to observe both the American and French customs. Each night we ate an appetizer, a main course, and dessert. Three weeks into our stay, Ian remarked that French cooking was an added benefit of accepting the position at Airbus. In Toulouse the meat, bread, vegetables, and fruit had more flavor. Most mornings, I walked half a mile to the street market and bought fresh farm products. On weekends, the four of us went to *le Marché Victor Hugo*, a nearby historic, covered market with stalls that sold premium fresh food like fish, meats, and cheeses. The extensive choices made it difficult to decide on our menu for that day and the next.

In terms of his work, Ian was the senior director for Flight Safety. To accommodate his position, a new department was created within *Aéroformation*, and Ian reported to Jean Pinet. Initially, Ian broadened his knowledge of the Airbus product. He had not flown an Airbus aircraft and followed the standard captain checkout in the A-320. Put into service in the spring of 1988, the A-320 was the first of Airbus 'fly-by-wire' aircraft. I asked Ian what his thoughts were on a computerized cockpit. He said the transition from regular flight controls to sidestick controllers was not difficult. The throttles that created speed margins for cruise and descent were now computerized. The multi-purpose-control-display-unit (MPCDU) operated the airplane in the autopilot mode. Before takeoff, a pilot loaded all current information into the device. Ian did not get a type rating, but he flew on several benign test flights, to record engine output and/or navigation display.

The above photo, taken August 11th, 1988, shows Ian in the reception hall of *Aéroformation*. He is talking to the editor of *Inter News*, an employee news bulletin. Ian spoke about his past career and described his new position. He said his focus would be diplomacy. He planned to effect changes within the organization and would ask for the cooperation of all departments. He spoke that August day about achieving cost efficiency without changing quality of service. He told the editor that as a leader, he emphasized communication.

I asked Ian about his typical work week at Airbus. He said Monday started with the *comité de direction* (Codir), a one to two-hour meeting of directors from various training departments, which included flight, maintenance, flight service, and engineers. The meetings were in English, the common language at Airbus. But only until an argument arose. Ian soon learned the French could argue only in their own language. On Tuesdays Ian visited the maintenance trainer and listened to instructors. Then on Wednesdays he sat through full simulator sessions. Thursdays were dedicated to meetings at the Airbus design office which, at the time, developed the A-321. This stretch-version of the A-320 had more powerful engines but few changes in the cockpit. Friday was usually a half day. On weekends, our family toured the countryside while Alec and Natasha recited (not by choice) French verb conjugations in the car.

The Airbus workforce impressed Ian. Long before Boeing began to manufacture aircraft sections in regional plants, Airbus had parts built in Germany, the United Kingdom, and Spain. The final assembly line was in Toulouse, where Ian met with the designers, engineers, and instructors. Some instructors were retired European pilots. Others had been seconded from an airline, with many from the United States and Canada. Airbus paid the airlines the pilots' salaries, a costly undertaking. There was no shortage of volunteers when word got around that Airbus was taking pilots on a one or two year temporary assignment in Toulouse.

The purchase of an Airbus aircraft included a contract for training five crews per airplane. Students came from airlines around the world, each with its own standards and manuals. Only after all training was completed could the airlines fly their newly acquired aircraft. This was an entirely new experience for Ian. At Pan American, he oversaw pilots hired for their flying experience. They were transitioning from one aircraft to another or upgrading to a higher position. A Pan American pilot who did not pass the required tests was fired. An Airbus trainee was not. The customer always came first. Airbus retrained failing pilots until they passed the tests. Yet the contract had a subclause that specified the number of extra training sessions before Airbus notified the airline and sent the pilot home. Ian determined the failure rate at one to two percent.

As the person in control of instruction, Ian coordinated the methods of teaching airplane systems. After reviewing courses, student feedback, and testing, Ian discovered weaknesses. He determined that half of the courses needed re-evaluation. Out of these meetings came the idea of a training symposium, conducted by *Aéroformation* for all past and future customers. Ian was the committee's chairman, and in November 1990, he presided over the first symposium in Toulouse.

Once Ian had received his official work permit, we became temporary French residents with French ID cards. This invalidated our Connecticut driver's licenses. The Airbus personnel office told Ian he had to take a full driver's course, pass a French written test, plus a driver's test. I offered to translate. But Ian refused my help and called the regulation, "ridiculous BS."

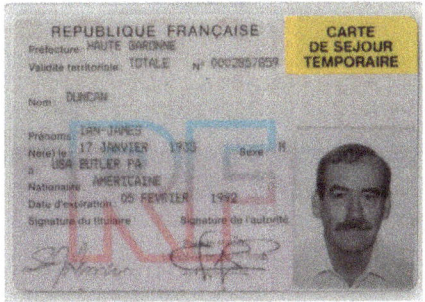

Ian's French identification card.

To learn more about obtaining the French license, I went to the *Préfecture de Police*. A clerk asked about my current license. I said it was American, issued in the state of Connecticut. He told me it was invalid. But he asked if I had any other license. I said I had a German one. *"Ah, celui-là c'est bon!"* I had almost forgotten about the folded, gray, oil-papered German license, so unlike the American laminated one. But I remembered the German license was issued for life. I told the clerk and said I would return. Walking home, I wondered where the license might be. In 1963 when it was issued, I was eighteen. Twenty-five years had passed. But to my surprise and joy, I located the license in a desk drawer, among expired German and U.S. passports.

Back at the *Préfecture*, I exchanged the German one for a French driver's license, which I learned was also good for life. When Ian heard this, he was jealous. The thought that a German driver's license was more valid than one from the United States infuriated him. He said he would not bother getting a French license. Fortunately, the police never stopped him.

By November of 1988, I felt relaxed and happy in Toulouse. The stress of moving and getting settled was over. Our new home looked beautiful. Pots with blue plumbago and orange hibiscus stood in our courtyard. Pink geraniums thrived in window boxes. In front of the guesthouse, a red bougainvillea twisted its branches through a wrought-iron trellis. In fall, it was cooler, and I often served dinner *al fresco*. Then one night Ian came home with big news. He grabbed a drink and wanted to talk at once. Before I could say anything, he told me he had been offered the position of V.P. Flight Operations at United Airlines.

At a loss for words, I slumped down on the couch.

"United wants me in Chicago," Ian said. "I'll get stock options and higher pay."

"You mean we're moving back to the States?" Then I recalled his earlier words, after he left Flight Operations at Pan American. "You said, Ian, that you would never work in that briar patch again."

He tried to appease me, said he had not accepted the position, and wanted to hear my opinion first. I tried to stay calm. Why did he need my input? Was I to decide for him? Nearly in tears, I said that I could not bear a move to Chicago. Ian agreed. He said he liked working at *Aéroformation* and preferred to stay in Toulouse. Yet, he might have accepted the position had we not come to France. The following morning, he called United Airlines and suggested Hart Langer, a friend from Pan American, as their V.P. Flight Operations. Hart accepted.

That fall we made friends in Toulouse and were invited to *soirées* and *dîners*. I hosted the traditional American Thanksgiving dinner and invited Jean Pinet, his wife Claudine, and another couple. Natasha said her first prayer in French. We feasted on fresh roasted turkey, one that had been cleanly plucked at a farm near Toulouse. There were the usual accompaniments, with pâté to begin, and a cheese and dessert course. Ian thought he had gone to heaven.

We entertained often. Guests enjoyed dining under our glass-covered dome. Serving a meal, even at the last minute, was not difficult in Toulouse. The butcher, baker, and grocer were close by. New and old friends, and Airbus customers dined at our home. Al Ueltschi, Flight Safety's president, came for breakfast or lunch upon arrivals in Toulouse. In 1989, Mrs. Heiman, the U.S. Consul General for the Southwest of France, visited the Airbus training facilities. She had dinner with us and stayed in the guesthouse.

In December 1988, we flew back to New York to spend the Christmas holidays with friends in Connecticut and Ian's sisters in New Jersey. Our original plan was to leave December 21st, fly from Toulouse to London and continue on Pan American's flight 103 to New York. Because flights were heavily booked on that date, we chose to travel a day earlier. On December 21st, we were with Bill and Viv in Connecticut when we heard that Pan American flight 103 had exploded over Lockerby, Scotland. Television news showed horrific images of aircraft parts scattered around the area. The thought that all four of us could have been on that fatal flight was so disturbing that I felt physically ill. Dispirited by the accident, Ian and I had little enthusiasm for a joyful holiday celebration. We returned to Toulouse before New Year's.

For the following two years, and on long weekends, we toured the South of France from the Atlantic to the Côte d'Azur. I took Alec and Natasha to Paris and London, and the four of us went by train to Berlin and Florence. Ian wanted to travel through Scotland. In summer 1989, we flew to Edinburgh for the annual festival, watched the Royal Military Tattoo, then rented a car. We made a circular seven-day tour to the highlands, the isle of Mull, Loch Ness, and back to Edinburgh. The visit included a day with Uncle Jimmy, Ian's last remaining Scottish relative, his father's younger brother.

Ian with Uncle Jimmy in Edinburgh, 1989.

Friends and family also came to Toulouse. Helen and Bob, plus Isobel and Phil, visited us on separate occasions. Jim, by then a pilot for Pan American, visited for New Year's in 1989. A few months later, he brought a Pan American stewardess he had been dating. Kim was tall, blond, and lovely. And she charmed us. Although she did not appear shy, later Kim told me she had been nervous and wanted to make a good impression. But to her dismay, on the flight from Paris to Toulouse, Jim had spilled coffee on her jacket. He would hear about this for years. We hardly noticed. Over lunch that day, Ian said to Jim, "You're right. She is the woman who brings joy to your eyes." Kim would become Jim's wife.

Then in July 1990, a bombshell.

M. Pinet announced that, as of October 1990, Ian would take charge of the Airbus training center in Miami. "Could we not move to Washington, D.C. instead? Any place but Miami," I said and told Jean Pinet how much the news had upset me. He apologized. But the announcement was *fait accompli*. Ian retired from Flight Safety. As Vice President of Technical Training, he worked under Airbus Industrie North America (AINA) and headed the Airbus Miami Training Center.

25

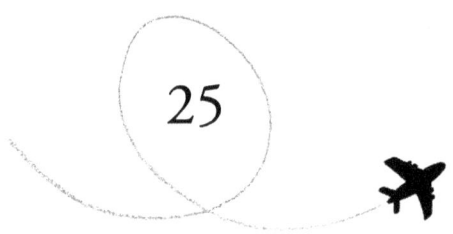

In October 1990, Ian relocated to Miami's Gran Vista at Doral and a furnished two-bedroom apartment. Airbus paid for the rental. Alec and Natasha needed to finish their third schoolyear, so we remained in France. Every other month, Ian came to Toulouse for *Aéroformation*. During school vacations, the children and I flew to Miami. Occasionally I joined Ian for a special event. As a retiree, Ian had retained his Pan American's travel privileges, which entitled us to free unlimited travel in first or business class.

The four of us celebrated Christmas 1990 in Toulouse, then visited Egypt over New Year's. I had booked the tour before Ian accepted the position in Miami, and before Iraq invaded Kuwait and triggered the first Gulf War. That December, I wondered if the conflict made travel to Egypt unsafe. Ian said we would be safer than ever. I trusted his optimism. We flew Egypt Air from Paris to Cairo, spent three days at the Hilton there. Alec wanted to climb a Giza pyramid until he realized its enormous height. Natasha and I rode a camel. We continued to Abu Simbel and Aswan where we boarded a ship to cruise north on the Nile. That winter, few tourists ventured to Egypt, which meant no waiting lines and crowds. The locals were friendly. As usual, Ian had been right. We never felt unsafe.

In July 1991, three years after we moved to Toulouse, our belongings were on their way to Miami. I sold our appliances to friends and donated the Weber grill we had converted to French propane. Alec, Natasha, and I stayed in a hotel during the final days. As for Sonya and her recently acquired French cousin, Gaspard, they were already in Florida. Early in June, both cats travelled first class on Pan American. Sedated, they slept during flight but woke up after Ian and I disembarked. The Siamese duo yowled a high-pitched duet. People stared as we walked through U.S. Immigration and Customs. As only Ian could, he made light of the situation and spoke to staring bystanders. He told them that one cat kept complaining about the food and the other had not liked the movie!

On July 10th, Alec, Natasha, and I left France. I felt deep sadness as our plane departed Blagnac. In the past three years in France, we had integrated into the local community, made friends, and called Toulouse our home. The children and I rarely conversed in English unless Ian was with us. On the flight from Paris to Miami, my thoughts went to the weeks ahead. How soon could I find a rental in Coral Gables? I knew nothing would compare to the house on *rue Agathoise*. But we would be reunited as a family and live in Ian's apartment until our shipment arrived. In the Miami airport, outside of Immigration and Customs, Ian welcomed me back with a large bouquet of flowers.

That summer, I enrolled Alec and Natasha in the French International Study program, which offered bilingual French/

American education in selected public schools. Half of their classes were in English, the others in French. We signed a lease on a house in Coral Gables and one year later we bought a home. That September of 1991, the four of us attended Kim and Jim's wedding in Annapolis.

Ian, Alec, Kim, Jim, Ilona, Natasha.

Ian and I made frequent trips to Toulouse. The first, on October 4th, 1991, was for the unveiling of the A-340. Around 5,000 dignitaries, officials, airline guests, and employees attended the grand event. *L'orchestre national et le choeur du Capitole de Toulouse* performed Carl Orff's *O Fortuna* as the first A-340 made its entrance into Aerospatiale's *Clément Ader* hangar.

The celebration coincided with the 20th anniversary of Airbus, now the world's second largest aircraft manufacturer. Outside the hangar, and as far as the runway, tents had been set up for a sit-down dinner. That night the champagne flowed, and international music groups entertained from three separate stages. The party lasted into the early morning hours.

The unveiling of the A-340 in Toulouse, France, 1991.

The week following the celebration, over 300 participants attended the second training symposium. Ian presided over the event. It lasted three days for 65 customer airlines. Although Ian was a gifted impromptu speaker and knew how to captivate an audience, he worked for days on his presentation. On one occasion, he was scheduled to give a speech during dinner and insisted that I teach him a few introductory French words. We practiced, "*Mesdames et Messieurs, bienvenue au symposium d'Aéroformation…….*" I was in the audience. People looked stunned. Before anyone could say something, Ian grinned and said, "Had you confused. You really thought I learned French!"

Ian at the podium of the Airbus Training Symposium.

Not long after our return to Miami, Ian was on an Air France flight back to Toulouse to welcome a delegation from the U.S. Federal Aviation Administration to Airbus.

For old times' sake, we spent Thanksgiving that year on the New Jersey shore. As in the past, Ian went duck hunting with his brother-in-law. I preferred to take a long stroll with Helen on the boardwalk. No one anticipated the shocking news a week later. On December 4th, 1991, Pan American World Airways ceased to exist. Ian lamented the loss and empathized with former employees. Son Jim immediately applied to fly for United and was hired. We wondered how the bankruptcy would affect Ian's retirement pay. For sure our travel benefits were over. But Ian quietly thanked Bob Gould for having done him an immense favor. Had Gould not fired Ian, he would be looking for work. I asked Ian if he had missed flying. After

Ian introducing the A-320 Simulator.

more than thirty years in the cockpit, he was happy to stay on the ground. But in case he ever had an overwhelming desire, he could always jump into a simulator.

26

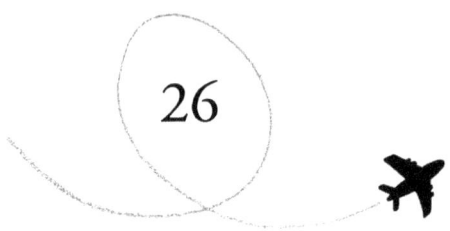

Ian held the Airbus fleet in high esteem, said the planes were safe and easy to fly. The first fly-by-wire aircraft, the A-320, had a set of multiple computers which the crew programmed. At the end of each flight, a self-monitoring system printed a report. An Airbus goal was to have a common cockpit. The instrumentation was the same in the A-320, 330, and 340. Even the simulators were interchangeable. The A-330's cockpit with two engines could be changed within two hours to an A-340 cockpit with four engines.

Unfortunately, the A-330's instrumentation did not supersede human error. On June 30th, 1994, an accident occurred in Toulouse during a test flight to certify the autopilot of a newer A-330 model, the A-330-321. The crew was to put the plane in automatic mode and simulate an engine failure after take-off. They took off manually and, at an altitude of 1,300 feet, pulled back one of the two throttles, simultaneously engaging the autopilot. They failed to realize that the autopilot was set to 2000 feet from the previous flight phase. The elevators commanded nose up. The plane, climbing at minimum speed immediately lost altitude and lateral control, then hit the ground. Three crewmembers and four observers died in the crash. The captain, Nick Warner, an Englishman, had been part of our social group in Toulouse.

Ian placed high importance on evaluating human error and teaching cockpit resource management. He studied each accident report, presided over Human Factor conferences. Years of experience served him well. In a 1996 speech during the Second Airbus Industrie Human Factor Conference, Ian emphasized the value of inquiry and advocacy in the cockpit. Failure to communicate and indecisiveness often ended in disasters. In later years, after his retirement from Airbus, Ian's expertise led to consulting engagements, and he joined Enders Associates International (EAI) for safety assessments which included the Hellenic Civil Aviation Authority in Greece and several U.S. airlines.

As an employer, Airbus took interest in its workforce, and under Ian's direction, employees at the Miami Training Center expressed contentment. All were invited to the annual Christmas gala at an upscale resort, or to board a luxury yacht and cruise Florida's intracoastal waterways. The black-tie event included a full bar, wine, champagne, dinner, and dancing. There was a gift for everyone: silk scarves, exclusive pen sets, and lottery drawings for free tickets on Air France to Paris. Ian said the events ran into six figures. In summer, a committee of employees organized the Airbus picnic, an all-day event for families and children at a resort. There were games, scavenger hunts, door prizes, swimming. No one left without a gift.

Airbus also treated their customers in style. Ian invited vice presidents of Flight Operations to join him on a three-day, all-expense-paid trip to fishing camps in Alaska and Canada, a male only event. My role was to stay home and wait for an overnight FedEx shipment of fish, to cook, marinate, or freeze them. Yet on one occasion, wives were invited. Ian and I with three other couples flew in a seaplane charter from Vancouver to a private floating camp in British Columbia's wilderness.

Ian with a King Salmon in Alaska.

There also were sporting events, which included skiing, fishing, and golfing. Wives were invited to the annual four-day retreat on one of the Hawaiian Islands with everything from helicopter rides to a day in the hotel's spa. I questioned these lavish invitations. Ian said Boeing, their competitor, did the same for their customers, even providing free travel on the Orient Express from London to Venice.

On the business side of things, the Miami Airbus center trained pilots from American, United, America West, Northwest, USAir, and also pilots from Venezuela, Mexico, Costa Rica, India, and Egypt. An important customer was Air Canada with its fleet of A-320s, A-330s, and 340s. The initial crews trained in Miami. Later the airline installed its own simulators. Ian befriended Captain B.W. MacLelland, Air Canada's V.P. of Flight Operations, and Air Canada's chief pilot, Captain Cam Bailey. Both men collaborated with Ian during the A-340 training phase. Every year, Ian and I received an invitation to Air Canada's Christmas party in Montreal, a lovely event at the *Auberge Le Saint-Gabriel,* the oldest inn in North America. The Bailey's have remained friends for life.

Although Boeing and Airbus were competitors, they attended Air Transport Association (ATA) meetings to exchange ideas about higher training efficiencies. Ian visited the Boeing training facility, and Boeing visited Airbus. Ian and I, along with other Airbus officials, attended the grand opening of Boeing's new training center in Seattle. During an ATA meeting in Bellingham, Washington, Boeing positioned their corporate yacht nearby and invited us for a long cruise with cocktails and hors d'oeuvres. Yet Ian had to tread carefully in his relationship with Boeing, and he doubted that Boeing broadcast its amicable cooperation with Airbus in the *Seattle Times.*

In the early 1990s, the Miami Airbus training center donated an A-300 trainer simulator to the University of North Dakota. The trainer had no motion but provided everything for a pilot to learn the

A-300's systems. Ian coordinated the transfer and met John Odegard, the founder and dean of the School of Aerospace Sciences. Over dinner, Odegard told Ian that U.S. college deans from Purdue, Florida International University, Embry Riddle, Western Michigan and Ohio State, all hoped to establish a Council on Aviation Accreditation. The plan was to give accreditation to colleges and universities with aviation departments. Would Ian agree to join the group? And in 1992, the Council on Aviation Accreditation (CAA) was established. A New Jersey lawyer, Jack McNamara, specialized in corporate and commercial aviation law, and he became the president. Ian served on its Board of Trustees as treasurer and CAA's corporate representative. Airbus allowed cash approval for transportation, hotels, and meals when Ian attended these affairs, which included hosting CAA members in Miami. The council met quarterly, had conference calls, and investigated flight programs.

In a letter to Ian, Jack McNamara recalled a heated debate during the CAA's initial meeting. Deans from various colleges could not agree. According to Jack, Ian accomplished what no lawyer, businessman, or dean could have. Ian's humorous quips made the attendees recognize their petty jealousies; and his tactful skill helped them arrive at a solution. Eventually, the dialogue Ian established between industry and academia, resulted in standards for universities with aviation programs. A student could graduate with an instrument, commercial, and instructor rating. The program worked so well that years later, the FAA allowed a student with five hundred hours, instead of the previous two thousand, to obtain an airline transport rating. Until his retirement in 1998, Ian served on the CAA's Board of Trustees.

In November 1992, Ian attended the 22nd International Federation of Airworthiness Conference in Long Beach, California; and as session chairman, he addressed the 45th annual International Air Safety Seminar.

Toward the end of his career, Ian was asked to join the Committee on Education and Training for Civilian Aviation Careers. The group, together with the National Research Council's Commission on Behavioral and Social Sciences and Education, created *Taking Flight: Education and Training for Aviation Careers,* a 160-page book published by the National Academy Press. In a letter dated April 19th in 1997, Bruce Alberts (chairman of the National Research Council) thanked Ian for his contribution, expertise, and commitment to the project.

That same month, Ian and I were invited to attend the Flight Safety Foundation's 50th anniversary dinner on April 8th at the National Air and Space Museum in Washington, D.C. Ian

received a laser-engraved wooden commemorative block.

Ian was in his late fifties when he told me he would retire at 62. A year before he approached his 62nd birthday, Ian notified Airbus of his planned retirement. The company tried to persuade him otherwise. As a compromise, Ian agreed to one more year, until January 1998. During these months, Ian developed a strategy for the location of a new training center. As Airbus sold more planes to countries in the Americas, the United States, Caribbean and Canada, the Miami Training Center became too small. Space allowed for only two full-flight simulators. Future growth would include two additional full-flight and four or five fixed base simulators. The old building, originally the headquarters for now defunct Air Florida, belonged to the Miami-Dade Airport Authority. Because Ian did not want trainees to drive 70 miles west to the Everglades or north to Fort Lauderdale, he hoped for a new location close to the Miami Airport.

The county commissioner, Natacha Millan, a smart Cuban woman, was supportive of Ian's idea. But who would finance the project? Ian wanted to secure a package deal, 10 million dollars for the building, plus 50 million for two additional simulators. Miami and Dade County officials did not believe the deal was worth the Airbus center's revenue. Yet Ian convinced them otherwise. Each year Airbus trained some 300 pilots, plus cabin crew and maintenance engineers from multiple airlines. The trainees needed hotels and food. They spent money, which according to Ian created 30 million dollars in annual revenue to the local community. In October 1997, the deal was signed. Airbus secured a 3.5 percent mortgage to finance the 60 million for the center and additional simulators. The new building would save the company 25 to 30 million

Dade County Mayor Alex Penelas signing the agreement in the presence of Captain Duncan and Natacha Millan.

in rent over the next thirty years. The location, 1.5 miles from the airport, two acres on 36th Street NW (a former Eastern parking lot), meant the entire development qualified for tax-free industrial bonds.

Ian retired while the construction was in progress, though we both attended the ribbon cutting ceremony and the inauguration.

In honor of Ian's retirement in January 1998, celebrations were held in Miami, Toulouse, and Washington, D.C. Senior management and dignitaries from many airlines attended the event in Washington's Army and Navy Club. The chief pilot of LACSA, Costa Rica's former airline, made Ian their captain for life. Dignitaries from Boeing, Flight Safety, and airline corporations brought gifts. United gave us two first class tickets to anywhere within their system. Boeing's Director of Training presented Ian with a leather flight jacket, its lining with the Boeing logo, and a handwritten card thanking Ian for his contribution to the airline industry, signed 'your friends from Boeing.' Jack McNamara, President of the CAA, presented Ian with a framed letter that included the following words:

> Because of you, ten thousand students will graduate each year, unwittingly, the beneficiaries of your efforts. Because of you, two hundred colleges and universities in the United States teach students in aviation degree programs, and now are aspiring to higher standards. A decade, hence, these students will serve millions of air travelers. Because of you, their flights will have arrived safely. No one will ever be able to sufficiently thank you. The entire membership of the CAA is proud to have been associated with you and are grateful you undertook this noble cause, and in doing so, inspired us to carry on.

Ian received hundreds of cards and letters. Ned Brown, the former director of Pan American's Training Academy, wrote: "In all my forty-five years in aviation, I have never met anyone who commands the respect and loyalty that you do. From the lowest rank to the highest, all know Jim Duncan as honest, with total integrity, who always knows what he is talking about. It has been a real honor to have served with you."

The college's President, Dr. Fitzpatrick, handing Ian his diploma.

Ian's career culminated on May 30th, 1998, with a Doctor of Science Honoris Causa from the College of Aeronautics, Flushing, New York.

The boy from Butler, Pennsylvania, son of poor Scottish immigrant parents, dreamed to soar blue skies, and in his aviation careers he reached a laudatory height. Mr. Phillips had the foresight to fund his education, and Ian's father unselfishly accepted the offer to remain Mr. Phillips' chauffeur. Mr. Scholter recognized Ian's exceptional work ethics at Butler-Graham Airport and suggested flying lessons. As Ian ventured into aviation, he displayed character and was driven to always do his best. As a leader, he hoped to make aviation a safer place. Yet with all the admiration, this great man remained humble. Ian's heroes were his parents, and his benefactor, and his mentor. He tried to live up to their expectations and to make them proud. I hope that in some mysterious way they shared in Ian's accomplishments, heard the accolades, witnessed his success.

Ainlie in America, I can hear his parents say. *We ur sae proud o' ye, laddie.*

Afterword from the Author

On the morning of August 24th, 2021, I walked into a hospital near Richmond, Virginia, with the hope of taking Ian home. Three days earlier, at our house in Wicomico Church, he had fallen and dislocated his hip. He had also been diagnosed with COPD and needed supplementary oxygen. Once again there were complications because of Covid restrictions and medical treatment.

That morning at the hospital, when I entered Ian's room, I saw his radiant smile. Overjoyed to see me, he said to the two nurses, "Meet my beautiful wife." Within fifteen minutes a physician arrived, and he told me that my husband was now a Hospice patient. The words barely sank in before Ian began gasping for air. I took his hand, told him to breathe and then, not more than a minute later, Ian was gone. There had been no time for an embrace, not even a minute for the two of us to be alone. I did know in my heart that Ian had waited for me to arrive so he could embark on a last flight. Only on this flight, and how painful to write these words, I was not joining him. Ian's rapid and sudden departure left me numb in a way I cannot describe. For over an hour, I stayed with him, wishing my husband of 47 years a fine landing wherever his final flight carried him.

As I write these words six months later, I find solace in a writer for whom Ian felt deep affection: the French aviator and author, Antoine de Saint-Exupéry. The following passage is from *Wind, Sand, and Stars,* and words Ian copied into his memorabilia folder.

Professional pilots are widely dispersed over the face of the earth. They land alone at scattered and remote airports, isolated from each other in the manner of sentinels between whom no words can be spoken. It needs the accident of journeying to bring together here and there the dispersed members of this great professional family. Round the table in an evening, at Casablanca, at Dakar, at Buenos Aires, we take up conversations interrupted by years of silence, we resume friendships to the accompaniment of buried memories.

Bit by bit, nevertheless, it comes over us that we shall never again hear the laughter of our friend, that this one garden is forever locked against us. And at that moment begins our true mourning, which, though it may not be rending, is yet a little bitter. For nothing, in truth, can replace that companion. Old friends cannot be created out of hand. Nothing can match the treasure of common memories, of trials endured together, of quarrels and reconciliation and generous emotions. It is idle, having planted an acorn in the morning, to expect that afternoon to sit in the shade of the oak.

So life goes on. For years we plant the seed, we feel ourselves rich; and then come other years when time does its work, and our plantation is made sparse and thin. One by one, our comrades slip away, deprive us of their shade.

I miss your shade, Ian, your love and support, your humor and wit. Now there are only memories of you to sustain me. Yet in these weeks and months since your departure, I have found consolation in the knowledge that the book we wrote together tells your remarkable story.

Ian and Ilona in Iceland, 2015.

www.ingramcontent.com/pod-product-compliance
Lightning Source LLC
Chambersburg PA
CBHW062045290426
44109CB00027B/2741